ROUND THE WREKIN IN KILOVERBS

By George Evans

Published by Plus Two Media Limited 2017

ROUND THE WREKIN IN KILOVERBS

First published in the UK in 2017

Published by
Plus Two Media Limited
Bridge Road · Wellington · Telford
Shropshire TF1 1RY
Tel: 01952 522562

ISBN: 978-1-5272-1837-6

Designed and typeset by: James Baylis
Plus Two Media Limited
www.plus2media.co.uk

Illustrations by: Jon Larter
www.scribbles-cartoons.co.uk

Printed and bound in the UK by: Stephens and George
www.stephensandgeorge.co.uk

A catalogue copy of this book is available from the British Library.

WHAT'S A KILOVERB?

Simply 1,000 words but don't tell Google, it doesn't know. What fun, we have a secret from the great Google.

I started the 'kiloverb' idea as a little game with myself while I was editing; it seemed fun so I kept it up. In the book I haven't tried to keep articles to 1,000 words and some of them are quite different.

WHAT'S THE BOOK ALL ABOUT?

Here are around 50,000 plus words about people, places and happenings in, on and around The Wrekin, mostly in Wellington, the largest town in the county of The Wrekin. (I can prove that's true if you like). We hope it will be interesting, thought provoking and fun. All the facts are as correct, honest and truthful as possible though some may appear quirky. What's wrong with quirky?

Over the last 90 years things have changed quite a lot; especially the looks of the folks but many of their ways are just as they were. People are people; they are all the same except that each is different. That's what makes them – and life - so interesting. This place and these people have changed a lot since 1923 and most of the changes feature in the book. Some of the new ways are much better or easier and some are not.

The 50 plus kiloverbs here have already been published in Wrekin (or Wellington) News over the last 17 years. Several readers have asked for a proper book to be published with some of the best articles included; here it is. James Baylis (of Plus Two Media Limited/Wrekin News), the publisher, and I hope you will enjoy it.

WHO IS GEORGE EVANS?

He's an old chap, born on Midsummer's Day in 1923 at 49, High Street, Wellington, Salop and has lived hereabouts ever since. Having taught for forty years and lived over 90 years in much the same place he is quite well known locally but is not at all famous anywhere else.

George is often asked, "You must have seen a lot of changes in and around Wellington." Yes he has and he's sure the changing lives of ordinary people in an ordinary unique town are much more interesting than all the tosh about kings and wars we were taught at school. Fortunately the teaching of history has improved, as have many things (though not everything) in the last 90 years. It's said that the past is another country and that must be true.

Despite living in much the same place during his long life George has not only seen, remembered and written about the huge changes to the people but has been able to influence quite a lot of them. He has been an office boy, soldier (and pacifist), student, teacher, youth leader, councillor, author of over 20 local interest books and How to be a Happy Old Man.

CONTENTS

"Can you imagine the lives of your own ancestors? Here's a book written by someone who lived through and can remember the changes to ordinary people"

01 INTRODUCTION

"History has an exciting future if it sticks to real subjects we understand, like our own environment. Then we may not keep repeating the old mistakes over again. History may have a bright future"

THE FUTURE OF HISTORY

When I was a boy history was very boring. It was simply a list of battles and kings and queens. Forgetting any battle, king or date was an offence often resulting in a caning. We learned, 'William, William, Henry, Stephen, Henry, Richard, John'; enough to keep us out of trouble for a while. The Battle of Bannockburn was fought on 24th June, 1314 but I only remember because I learned it on my birthday, 24th June, while changing age from 13 to 14 and I still don't know who won. Nor did I ever care.

The next fashion came. Children were expected to have interesting opinions about many aspects of history without any idea what had happened. Their casual thoughts were considered far more important than any hard facts – at least by a few trendy teachers. That was a silly time and only happened in a few schools, though the media fulminated mightily about it. That's what sells newspapers. Those of us who thought we knew better carried on doing what we thought right.

Then there were the 'topics' and 'projects', which sensible teachers juggled around until the syllabus had some relevance to real life, and in particular to the lives of those in the class. All attempts to make history sensible were attacked by 'experts' with entrenched ideas and often little experience of teaching. Some of us taught for forty years without ever being trendy. 'Educational Experts' are often suspected of being failed teachers.

Now, according to my great grandchildren, history at their schools is interesting to them. They don't learn lists by rote and the way Romans really lived here is more important than who the emperor was. They are fascinated by different ways of life and changing priorities and find history is interesting' not boring or confusing. Hurrah for their teachers! They may never become historians but at least they are learning to understand their environment in terms of time and evolution as well as in space through geography.

Local history is so much more real than the old textbooks because we live with the results of previous happenings. It's not just Blists Hill, Sunnycroft and Wroxeter; it's Watling Street/ Holyhead Road, The Wrekin and Market Square, not to mention recent changes to places all around us, even brash new Telford.

Local history is the real thing; it's what we all understand and are interested in. Come to think of it, all history of any kind is local somewhere. Our old Wellington is packed tight with history. That's why Wellington History Group works so hard to discover and publicise it.

It used to be true that the only thing we learn from history is that mankind learns nothing from it. That's true of the old-fashioned stuff but there's now hope. History has an exciting future if it sticks to real subjects we understand, like our own environment. Then we may not keep repeating the old mistakes over again. History may have a bright future.

LOCAL KNOWLEDGE

Feeling part of the community we live in is important. That's easy for us natives but needs effort from newcomers. 'That's when good neighbours become good friends'. Understanding local history and the environment brings a respect for the place we live.

Children should learn about their environment at school. For many years I have practised and advocated teaching local studies in schools, involving history, geography, ecology, religions and a lot of enjoyable visits to places of interest. It's particularly easy in our area, where there have been momentous historic happenings and such varied geography; hills, plains, rivers, forest, farmland, industry and people from all over the world. Children quickly absorb a sense of belonging to the community and think of themselves as part of it. They soon adopt the local accent and accept local customs.

For adult newcomers it is worth while making the effort to learn about the place they now inhabit and the people with whom they share it. Most folks living 'round The Wrekin' are friendly and welcoming provided their new friends don't harp on about somewhere else being better than here. We think this is the best place in the world to live. Accept that and you're one of us; otherwise please go somewhere else.

Telford is rightly criticised for lacking social organisations but all the established towns and villages here are full of them. There many ways of integrating comfortably into a community. One is to join a religious group. I'm a Quaker and have been welcomed to most of the churches and other religious groups in this area. Or join a political party; they'd be glad to see you. Supporting the local team is another way of joining in or frequenting a good pub. Most games are played here, so join in if you want. We all know many people now have to move around the country – and the world – to get promotion. Many local people were born somewhere else, settled here and are completely accepted.

Children, of course, are always newcomers. However, they can integrate more rapidly than adults. Those arriving with no English frequently learn more quickly in the playground than in the classroom. Adults take longer and have to work harder. Those who learn to understand and appreciate their new environment are the most integrated and certainly seem the happiest. Longing to go back where you came from, especially when it's not possible, is condemning yourself to unnecessary misery, so is desperately trying to turn your new home into a replica of the old one.

So how do you learn about the environment around The Wrekin? I have written 20 local books on the subject and Allan Frost has probably published more. Neil Clarke, Geoff Harrison and several others have also produced excellent work, though they are difficult to buy these days. Anyway, most of my books and some of Allan's are sold out, though of course there should be copies in Wellington Library. It may amuse readers to know that the first commercially published book about Wellington was, 'Wellington in old Picture Postcards', published by a Dutch company called European Library in 1987; I wrote it. It was officially the top selling book in Telford - jointly with Rushdie's 'Satanic Verses'. Rushdie made more money – and much more trouble – than I did!

For those of us with access to the net there are many other opportunities to access information about local history. Several excellent websites give a wealth of knowledge and some, such as Wellington History Group will allow you to download and print off their magazines. Wellington

Town Council (make sure it's our Wellington, not Somerset or New Zealand) have their own version and Wellington LA21 (Local Agenda 21, a local conservation group), which has recently published a new and excellent small magazine on their 'Five Towns Trail' has also a great website. Wellington H2A is another fine website; they're the people who organise the 'Summer Fayre', Wrekin Barrel Race and a lot of entertainment in Market Square. They're young, exciting and reliable at the same time.

A word of warning; do beware of websites not locally based. Shropshire Tourism said that Wellington had a street market until we pointed out that the biggest and best market in the county had its own premises and was not in the street. Wikipedia once stated that Wellington was on the Welsh border! If it's not run by local people – suspect it.

Wellington History Group not only publishes a series of magazines called Wellingtonia, edited by Allan Frost and written by all of us; we also give a series of history lectures in Wellington Civic Centre. Keep an eye open for the next programme. Come early to get a seat, they're popular. There are increasingly more local history organisations in the other towns and villages in The County of The Wrekin. We are looking forward with increased confidence to the opening of The Wrekin Museum, perhaps in Edgbaston House.

Perhaps the best way to learn about the locality is to go and look for yourself. There are Town Walk leaflets to help you, but go and ask and see and wonder. This is the way those of us who write the books found out and if you think we know it all, then think again. I've only been exploring this town for 87 years so I've a lot to learn.

But however much we locals try to help, you'll have to make an effort for yourself. If you have skills and enthusiasm please join.

There's going to be a much better library opening soon in those wonderful new buildings near the swimming pool and Civic Centre. This will have a dedicated area for community studies and all of us interested in the town, The Wrekin and its environment are getting very excited about this new facility. It will need volunteers to help with the provision of information. Would you like to help? If so, keep an eye open for news.

SHOP LOCALLY

SUPPORT YOUR OWN TOWN

We are often told gloomy news about the plight of British town centres. We're urged to 'do something about it' and all sorts of experts who know how trends are going pontificate about what Government and Big Business should do. The other day I met an old friend who said the usual, "Poor old Wellington, it's not like it was, is it?" I asked whose fault she thought that was and she was surprised at the question. I asked how often she went into Wellington (she does live here) and she thought she hadn't been for several years. So I said, "Then it's your fault isn't it?" We're still friends.

When you think about it you realise that our local shopkeepers are well worth supporting and that it's in our own interests to at least try very hard to keep them going. All the ones I know are, in their own way, the salt of the earth. At least those who are most successful are. They provide a service to us as well as simply selling goods. They are also a friendly bunch of people, if for no other reason than that it is in their interests to be.

If you go to a city it is quite usual to find the businesses bright, brash and soul-less. The 'town centre' of Telford is going that way and I find it unfriendly. Telford's shopping centre is a copy of an American out-of-town shopping mall. Despite the efforts of some of its workers it is a miserable place. Its shops seem dictated to by their Head Offices, with not enough responsibility given to their local managers and staff and no understanding that towns are different from each other.

Oh dear, I'm going to be accused of another bit of Telford bashing though I find Telford a building site with delusions of grandeur. It's run by the money men with little concern for their customers rather like our main banks. It's not the fault of the good people who work there but of all the head offices where the money grubbers dictate to the branches.

Back to local towns, with real town centres, full of character and actually wanting to provide a service for their customers. "Ah!" Some will say, "But I can't get what I want from there." My answer to that is that, apart from a couple of short holidays, I can honestly say that for the last three years I haven't bought anything from any shop outside Wellington.

While I think about it, apart from my wedding ring (from Shrewsbury 63 years ago) I'm not wearing anything that didn't come from Wellington market; that includes my shoes, watch and wallet. My glasses and dentures also came from Wellington. So don't say I never practise what I preach.

Thinking of all the odd things I've needed lately – a gas cooker, Santa Clause outfit, camera, knife sharpener, Christmas cards, medicine, bank, butcher, supermarket, pipe tobacco, eggs, copy of Wrekin News, weather-proof coat, carpet, duvet cover, plant markers for the Peace Garden, warm trousers, telephone, torch, belt, vacuum cleaner, wine, lamp, rug…I could go on for ever but they all come from Wellington – mostly from the market.

There are many advantages in buying locally, one of the most important being that if anything's wrong (perhaps your own fault) there's a friendly person who will sort it out. Then it's not far to go and petrol is expensive, and there's no parking charge to worry about. A while ago I had a problem with a vacuum cleaner I bought in the market. It wasn't Graham's fault but he not only replaced the part quickly and efficiently but also collected and delivered it. Would that have happened if I'd bought it online? I think not.

There's one thing wrong with Wellington though – we don't have a bookshop that sells new books. There's an excellent second-hand bookshop in the market, kept by Rob, one of the best I have ever seen. Go and buy a book from him. Between them, WH Smith and Menzies destroyed the two excellent bookshops that we had – Jenny Smith in the market and Vision Books in Market Square. Having spoiled their rivals' trade by undercutting on all the most profitable lines, like best sellers and text books, the 'big boys' have abandoned our town. In both cases the local staff was helpful and easy to work with but constantly overruled by their head offices.

Please will someone now start up a book shop in our town? I know the supermarkets sell some books but they don't seem interested in the kind I want to read. I can buy them in Much Wenlock, Church Stretton, Ludlow or Bridgnorth but why not in Wellington? You can buy a copy of Allan Frost's latest on line, but not in the town he's writing about. Wellington has the biggest and best free Literary Festival in Britain but we don't have a bookshop! Well, that's my grumble over.

It's great to see Dawley folk beginning to realise that they have a unique culture of language, full of wit and fun. I'm a Wellington man but I admit that Dawley does 'talking broad' better than we do. Oakengates (once 'the brightest little town in Shropshire') has its own attractions as has the ancient town of Madeley, which pre-dates Ironbridge by maybe a thousand years. The villages of Ketley and Hadley have their shopping and business centres too. If you don't want to lose them – use them.

Buy local whenever you can. Support the real town centres. Make it a social occasion; meet friends and neighbours. Enjoy free parking, a coffee, a library book or a swim. In any good traditional town there are many extra facilities and shopping or simply visiting them is a pleasure. We customers have the power when we care to use it. Our local traders treat you as a friend; let's treat them as friends.

FAMILY HISTORY

A CAUTIONARY TALE

The tales and traditions of families are not always as they might seem. Beware of assuming that ancient stories are non-fiction.

Some time ago I wrote a little story about my Fail grandfather. It was published in Wellington News. A family researcher spotted his unusual surname and sent me more information that really surprised me. He had always claimed to be descended from a Scottish family, previously named McPhail, though he had been born in Chester. According to the records, however, the facts were that his family came from Northumberland, not Scotland. I had never imagined that the Scottish story could be untrue; he was such an upright sort of man who would never dream of telling a lie. I can only suppose that he believed what he told me.

My other grandfather, when asked his age, always used to say, "As old as my tongue and a bit older than my teeth". He would never deviate from that. When he died the family found his birth certificate and his parents' marriage certificate; they both gave the same date. Did his mother really get married on the day she was giving birth to her son? This time it's the official records – or at least one of them - that I don't believe.

The classic joke is about the professional family researcher who charged £100 for looking up records and £1,000 to keep quiet about them.

When it comes to family legends; it ain't necessarily so!

"As old as my tongue and a bit older than my teeth"

A SEAT IN THE SQUARE
TALES AND HISTORY ABOUT WELLINGTON TOWN CENTRE

The other day I sat down in Market Square (Market Place if you like) and it occurred to me that I had a kiloverb (1,000 words) of history and memories to tell about the view from where I sat. My bench was on the west side, so I looked east; the view stretched from Station Road across to the bottom of New Street.

We go left to right. First there's Station Road, about where the Talbot Inn used to be before the railway came in 1859 (no, I don't remember; don't be cheeky). The Talbot was the premier hotel in Wellington and where local government had been transferred after the demolition and sale of our market hall.

Then comes HSBC, which was built as the North and South Wales Bank, later to become the Midland Bank. My grandfather, John Evans, kept his money there and introduced my father, as was the custom, when he was 21.

My earliest memories of the Midland Bank were of a huge wooden counter, about six feet wide and 20 or 30 feet long. Behind it were several bank clerks – all men – wearing black jackets and waistcoats, striped trousers, stiff white collars and dark ties. The atmosphere was dark, quiet and solemn. There was no queue and none of the protection afforded to modern staff. All transactions were meticulously recorded in books using 'dipper' pens and proper ink.

In 1923, to 'start me off in life', I was given a small savings account by my grandfather, so I later became their oldest customer. As a young teacher with a wife and family to support I often found myself with 'too much month left at the end of my money', which I explained to the manager, so he allowed me an overdraft of no more than next month's pay cheque.. A few years ago, however, I transferred to another bank. This was no fault of the staff there but because 'head office' had cut their numbers too far for them to be able to cope with anything slightly unusual. I do like the cupola above the building and think it is a little gem.

Next, and really part of the same building, are the cash points (holes in the wall), often very useful. This was WH Smith's shop, later becoming an office of the Ordnance Survey when huge changes were being made in the maps of Telford. Presumably the OS now use aerial surveys so their offices don't need to be near the place they're mapping.

Then there's the place we remember as the Square Café, kept originally by Giuseppe Sterlini. His is a sad tale of the stupidity of war. Because he was born in Italy he was an 'enemy alien' so he had to report regularly to the police – with a jug of coffee. Eventually he was deported to Canada, though his only crime was being born in the wrong country. The evacuation ship was sunk by the Germans and he, like many others, was drowned. His wife and daughters kept the excellent café going for many years. There's a new one just starting that seems to be concentrating on chicken; I wish it well.

The next shop was a lovely shoe shop not long ago and should have thrived. We've no idea why it didn't, for all the excellent ideas and very hard work of its owner. It should have succeeded. Now it's Newsline, presumably taking over some of the business done by the recently departed WH Smith. Long ago this was Bates and Hunt's chemist shop, where I always thought Dr William Withering's father was a pharmacist and William was born. I've been sternly told I mustn't say this because I can't prove it. So I can't, but who can prove me wrong?

Next door is Seatons' sportswear shop, where I bought my last pair of walking boots as an 80th birthday present for myself. They have lasted so well I decided not to get another pair for my 90th. They seem to cater for most sports and have arrangements with clubs, though not ever having been 'sporty' all I know is that they sell excellent walking gear.

Long, long ago this was run by a Mr Capsie as a very high class ladies' dress and hat shop. There my mother went in 1902 as an apprentice dressmaker and learned her trade very well indeed. In those days her father had to pay Mr Capsie to teach her, in spite of the fact that she worked for him.

In front stands a much more recent addition – our Community Clock. This came about in 1999 after a lot of work by Town Councillor Gary Davies to celebrate the millennium. Money was raised by public subscription and we all contributed. Later, when the Market Square was being remodelled, the Town Council voted to move the clock to Larkin Way but a huge outcry from the 'owners' who had subscribed persuaded the council to keep it in the Square. As an interesting addition to the sets of the Square there are small iron plaques built in to mark the position of the old Market Hall, which was demolished around 1800; do find them.

In fairly recent years Seatons' shop was Vision Books, run by Steve Ellis. He was doing very well until the 'big boys' of the bookselling world ganged up on him. They took all his 'best sellers' and school books and heavily discounted them, driving the poor chap out of business. It was a lovely shop and I do wish it could come back; we need a bookshop selling new books. Steve also published three of my books, all of which sold well. Now there's nowhere to sell any new books written by local writers – of whom we have several very good ones.

Oh Dear! I have run out of space and have to stop.

"I often found myself with too much month left at the end of my money"

02 WELLINGTON

THANK YOU WELLINGTON

On Midsummer's Day last it was my 90th birthday. This, I have to say, was a bit of a surprise. I had never expected to live this long and there were times, especially about two or three years ago when I really didn't want to. Mind you it was also a nice surprise to have arrived at my 22nd birthday considering what had happened since my 21st. Then the German Army, their Air force, the American Air force, the RAF, and the Royal Artillery had all had a go at me – and they all missed. So much for military efficiency.

So I began to wonder who I should thank for helping me to live, mostly happily, for the last 90 years. The more I wonder about this, the more people I realise are responsible. First there's my parents, who handed over a reasonably good set of genes. This was crucial as there are plenty of genetic problems I didn't inherit. Of course that means I have to thank their parents and ancestors back a lot of generations. There are others, including the medics who repaired my dad after he was shot and the sailors who rescued my mum when she was shipwrecked; they all earned my gratitude.

Talking about health, there's the Rechabite friendly society, one of many such groups which paid the doctors' bills for their members before the National Health Service was started. I had bovine TB, which might well have killed me 85 years ago if we hadn't been able to pay the doctor.

Still on medical matters, there have been several occasions when I have been rescued and patched up by the NHS. There was an ulcer, a couple of broken ribs and a nasty fall on The Wrekin that caused a dent in my skull for instance. All these could have polished me off but for the good old NHS. We may grumble about it at times but how many old chaps of my age are still here by kind permission of the NHS? I suspect the answer is most, if not all of us.

That's a bit about the physical side of my survival; the rest is concerned with my need for family and friends. No man is an island; we humans are a species that tends to flock together and to co-operate in order to survive. Although I was an only child and have always quite enjoyed my own company I do need a little help from my friends. I wouldn't make a good hermit or a Trappist monk. For their friendship I need to thank the whole town of Wellington, where I have lived since coming into the world, and everybody who has lived here. Of course some have to be thanked more than others but I'm not daft enough to name them because it might hurt some who must be left out. Wellington is a particularly friendly town and I do hope it will continue like that. The increase in its multi-ethnic complexion seems not to have changed this aspect of the town's character at all.

Growing up in High Street was quite an experience, though I don't remember much. Years later I met two old ladies who remembered me being born, and that I was a remarkably fat baby. My mum's helper pushed me all round town in my pram and then she took me for walks when I was old enough. I remember Peacock's Penny Bazaar in the market where you could buy little toys for 1d and a woman who sold cheese and would gouge out a sample to taste with her long black thumbnail. There was a chap who sold china and would break some to gain everyone's attention. On Mondays there were often cattle or sheep being driven to the Smithfield market wandering or even running about the streets. Best of all, she pushed me up The Wrekin in my perambulator with some of my family. Before I was four I was sent to Constitution Hill Infants' School, where the teacher was surprised I could already recognise most of the letters and could read a bit.

Later on I have to thank the staff at Wellington Boys' High School (now part of New College) for broadening my education and to my classmates for their friendship as well as those who introduced me to Scouting, which was very good fun. Although the school was fiercely strict it didn't stop us enjoying ourselves, sometimes with a little mischief.

After school there was work at Allied Ironfounders in Ketley and Joseph Sankey's Hadley works, for introducing me to office life. At the same time there was Walker Technical College and the Home Guard, where we defied Hitler's forces after work. Then I was 'called up'. There's very little to thank the Army for – I hated it, especially for the eleven months when I was being shot at. There was one thing, however, for which I can thank them; that's for introducing me to teaching, first to adults and then children.

On returning to England I taught at Craven Arms and Wistanstow before college; that was a total of three years which I wouldn't have survived without my parents' help, a bit of savings and living a simple life.

My next helper was my wife, Naomi, who helped me more than anyone else for over sixty years. She and my lovely family are those to whom I am most grateful.

Suddenly I realise there are many others I have left out who should be included but that it would take me into thousands more words than I am allowed in this article. There's the hundreds of friends I have taught at Prince's Street and Orleton Park, the Explorers at Bennet's Bank, the councillors of the Wellington UDC and Town Council, the Civic Society, AFRTW, Museum Partnership, History Group, Youth Hostellers, neighbours and friends. Goodness, what a lot!

Thank you, Wellington; please keep it up a while longer.

WELLINGTON URBAN DISTRICT COUNCIL - SOME MEMORIES

For many years the town of Wellington was administered by its own Urban District Council, which took over from the Commissioners in 1894; the Civil Parish was divided between Wellington Urban and Wellington Rural District Councils. These were abolished in 1974 when the Wrekin District Council was formed. That too disappeared in 1998 when The Wrekin District was removed from Shropshire and became the county of The Wrekin. The appropriate law is an Order titled 'the Shropshire (District of The Wrekin) (Structural Change) Order 1996', which came into force on 1st April 1998.

The Urban area was roughly what we now think of as the town and the Rural Council dealt with the villages around, though Hadley and Ketley cannot be described as rural areas and were, for most of the time heavily industrialised. The RDC also had Parish Councils which met separately, taking responsibility for some functions and making recommendations to the RDC on others.

The UDC had many responsibilities, including public housing, slum clearance, parks, allotment gardens, roads, parking, water supply, sewerage and sewage disposal, public lavatories, road safety, street cleaning and lighting, refuse collection and disposal, public health, swimming baths and trading standards. Overall town planning was a County Council function, as was education, police and the Fire Brigade though the UDC made frequent recommendations about their own patch. In fact the UDC had many more duties than the present Telford and Wrekin Borough Council as some have been delegated to bodies like the Severn Trent Water Board, The UDC thought of itself as being responsible for pretty well everything that went on in the town and was often forward-looking, seeking ways of improving trade, housing, leisure and living standards. Councillors, however, kept a keen eye on expenditure.

There were 15 councillors; five being elected each year, all for the whole town until wards were introduced in the 1960s. Many were independent and those belonging to political parties promptly forgot their party allegiances after the election, concentrating on what they as individuals thought was best for the town and never meeting as a caucus. I was asked to 'put up' for the council in 1954 and very reluctantly did so after a promise that no-one would ever tell me how I must vote on any subject.

Election day came and I found, to my surprise, that it was quite exciting. To begin with I had not particularly bothered whether I was elected or not and looked forward to losing and getting on with life as before; as the day came nearer there was a little frisson of excitement. Is this common to councillors today? Eventually there was the count and I found myself, as in the two next elections, bottom of the five elected. As usual only around 30% voted.

We met in Walker Street and I found the others friendly and supportive, asking what committees I wanted to be on. They were a dedicated group of (mainly) independents with (mostly) Conservative leanings. There was no hint of party meetings; it was 'every man for himself'. At my first Council meeting I established my credentials as one of the 'awkward squad' when the reservoir was reported 30 feet down and I asked how far it was up.

From there on there was a seemingly endless ritual of evening meetings and my little son learned to say, "Daddy 'genda" as the big envelopes clunked through the letterbox. The council took up most of my 'free' time for nine years. Why do it? I wondered. I wanted to influence the development of Wellington and perhaps, to a very small extent I did but not as much as I would have liked.

We had no party meetings. An annual pre-council informal meeting decided who should be on which committee and who should be chairman and vice-chairman of the council. This was agreed on the principle that each councillor should take his turn provided he has at least three years experience. Parties, gender and age were nothing to do with it.

There were some interesting characters on the council; brewers, undertakers, accountants, industrialists, civil servants, shopkeepers, wholesalers, and assorted retirees. The speed record for a full meeting, including the usual forty pages of committee reports was 12 minutes. Spending £250,000 on a sewage disposal plant took 2 minutes but deciding to buy the rent collector a new bike took half an hour. An argument about how to deal with the debts of a recently 'retired' clerk was defused by, "I thought we were supposed to be Christians".

The most expensive items were council houses, of which we owned 2,000 by the end of my stint. It was a hugely expansive time, as Arleston, North Road, Hollies Road estates and so on were developed and private firms like Fletchers were building too. This was the post-war housing boom.

In 1961 I found myself elected Chairman and first citizen of my town. At my first council meeting Cllr. Ernie Griffiths challenged my ruling and I had to tell him to sit down and be quiet as he was 'out of order'. With the chair came an ex officio appointment as magistrate and that was interesting. The first thing I was advised was to be quiet and learn. I learned that though some spoke the truth, nobody spoke the whole truth and some spoke anything but the truth; also that I was unsuited to the job.

We (Naomi my wife, Reuben Rushen the clerk and I) decided there should be a civic reception, which became a dinner. It's satisfying that the Town Council revived it in 1988, after the fourteen years Wellington was without its own council. To make sure everyone wanted to come we made it difficult to get a ticket and charged a high price. Profits went to charities.

Recently there have been proposals to once more change the system, this time to a 'unitary' authority incorporating both Shropshire and T&W Councils. Will that actually happen?

WELLINGTON TOWN CENTRE WALK 2023

WELLINGTON HAS CHANGED OVER THE LAST TEN YEARS. This is quite normal of course; it's no longer the 13th Century market town, nor the East Shropshire railway junction of 19th century. Like any other settlement worth its salt, Wellington has always changed to adapt to fresh situations and fashions. Our town centre has reversed the decline caused or exacerbated by the Telford Development planners and their successors.

So let's go on a walk and spot ten years of changes. We start at the Civic and Leisure Centre which began the move of emphasis from shopping to community use. The library is now having to increase staff to cope with extra numbers of readers and the use of the swimming and exercise facilities has rapidly expanded. Regular events at the Peace Garden have meant more business for the café. The new Wrekin link has enabled walkers to park in town and be magically transported to the start of their walk.

The old library is now an exciting museum of The Wrekin, with user-friendly exhibits on The Wrekin Forest and the towns and villages of East Shropshire.

The move of Further Education into the centre has also increased use. New College has moved its Fine Arts and Music departments into the old YMCA and Post Office buildings, making adult classes more popular. Frequent concerts in Market Square provide entertainment for all and performance practice for musicians and other artists. Many more people are now living above the shops, further increasing the footfall for the small specialist shops, cafes pubs and restaurants.

Looking from Church Street we see the pedestrian link between Bus Station and Railway Station and the multi-storey car park accessed from the Parade that now occupies the old bay's site and its platforms. Barclays Bank is demolished, giving access to the wonderful gardens and pool created on the site of the old bus garage, where the medieval town pond used to be. This is yet another attraction for tourists, who are greatly helped by the new Information Centre on the site of WH Smith's.

We now go down Market Street, where the fine old market continues to flourish and has joined in the town's increased prosperity. Across Bridge Road is the Clifton with its new function as an important Arts Centre, having well used facilities for a specialist cinema, a theatre and for many performances both during the day with Wrekin College, New College, Telford College and some of the local secondary schools during daytime and both amateur and professional events in the evenings. Many of those who doubted its use now complain of their difficulty in getting tickets.

So now we're back at the Civic Centre and wondering which of Wellington's new developments to investigate first. More investment has resulted in increased prosperity, benefiting everyone except pawnbrokers, charity shops and money-lenders, all of whom have now become specialists in other fields. 'To Let' signs are now rare. The town has undergone a mini-revolution. Hurrah!

WELLINGTON AND THE WREKIN

Wellington is The Wrekin's town and The Wrekin is Wellington's little mountain. This, I think sums up the relationship between the two. Marc Petty asked me to write a kiloverb (1,000 words) about this subject, which I have summed up in 12 words and could easily fill an encyclopaedia about. If I didn't know – and feel – a great deal about the subject it would be easier to write about it. It's an emotional bond between the people and their environment that has so many different aspects. Over the millennia the people have changed many times, sometimes violently due to conquests and often due to more peaceful changes.

Let's begin around three thousand years ago; it was a time of climate deterioration, with failed crops and consequent frictions and wars. A refuge was built on top of The Wrekin – its hillfort. People could more easily defend themselves and their families there, though between battles they had to go to the farmlands below to grow their food. Then The Wrekin meant safety.

Hundreds of years later the Iron Age Celts came and with their superior technology, dominated the land, extending and improving the fortifications.

Gradually, over the centuries the role of the hillfort changed. Its main functions were as a base for the warriors and leadership/administration, and also as a sacred mountain for the priests. The Roman invaders are credited with introducing civilisation. One can only remark that military dictatorship, slavery and heavy imperial taxes were their main imports; most of their technology had been in Britain long before. Their new town, Viroconium, is clearly named after The Wrekin and had views that a modern estate agent would say improved the selling price of a house.

After a brief stint as capital of Britannia the British/Roman administration collapsed until the Angles arrived and took over the area. They too named places after The Wrekin, including Wroxeter and Wrockwardine, making it clear that they respected the little mountain in their own way. By then most local people had Angle, Roman, Celtic and pre-Celtic ancestors.

This seems a good time to think about the origins of The Wrekin's name. The oldest language we have currently is Welsh or more politely Cymraeg. Their name is Gwrygon or something like that, but unlike most Welsh place names it doesn't mean anything in their language. Most Welsh hills' names have a perfectly sensible or mythical meaning. This does not, which suggests to me that it is from the even earlier language of pre-Celtic people.

Danish and Norse raids left no permanent mark except a few names like Norton. We should suspect that the local folks, having no means to fight a Danish raid, ran off into The Wrekin Forest. With the temporary border between the Danelaw and Saxon Law established as Watling Street, Wellington was for a while in a different country to The Wrekin.

No sooner had life settled down and the Anglo-Saxons established themselves as the English when perhaps the most arrogant invaders came – the Normans. By brutal terrorism they, though few in number, dominated the country. They even called The Wrekin Mount Gilbert after a Norman hermit who seems to have done nothing in a most religious way. Wellington became known as Walitone and later The Wrekin was named 'Gilberti Mons'. Later the English language replaced Norman/French and life became a little more civilised.

What is the origin of Wellington? There are several theories put forward by historians like the place of the temple in the grove or the settlement of a Saxon called Wella or even the place of wells. My favourite idea is that the Domesday name, Walitone, might be correct and that like Walcott and Wall it means the place of the Welsh. Actually the word Welsh is an early English insult but most Welsh people seem as happy to live with it as modern Quakers do with their name.

Gradually Britons, Celts, Romans, Angles, Saxons, Danes and Normans blended together and became English. One day, perhaps soon, DNA analysis will become more popular and we shall be more able to piece together our various ethnic origins; perhaps we shall find that we 'natives' have ancestors from all the peoples who have, legally or illegally, through conquest or as economic migrants, settled here. Hello cousin!

Since the last World War a great assortment of people have come to the lands around The Wrekin; Poles, Yugoslavs, Germans, Italians, Afro-Caribbeans, Indians, Pakistanis and Chinese in particular. It's interesting to watch them settling down, bringing their own contribution to local culture and absorbing local habits including a love of The Wrekin.

Fortunately none of these latest arrivals has tried to conquer us and as Wellington is generally a friendly place almost all are settling in well. One Pakistani friend told me years ago that he had 'gone native'. It should never be thought that one cannot be a Wellingtonian unless, like me, they were born here; it is enough to want to be Wellingtonian.

We happily share our little mountain with Hadley, Dawley, Ketley and all other Friends round The Wrekin – even some Shrewsbury people! The local toast to All Friends Round The Wrekin was described as an ancient tradition as long as three hundred years ago; do learn it and use it at the slightest excuse.

Nowadays visitors and families favour the direct route – the Pilgrims' Way – to the top, often picnicking. Exercisers shave seconds off their 'best time'. Thoughtful explorers marvel at the geological variety and the triumph of natural forest regeneration. Regulars find solitude, peace and spiritual comfort.

The Wrekin and its forest attract large numbers of walkers every fine day but there's more to it than many dream of. One poet, Jim Hatfield, likened The Wrekin to Japan's Fujiyama as a sacred mountain.

WALKER STREET
THOUGHTS AND MEMORIES

Walker Street has been changed recently. It used to extend from where the Taj Mahal restaurant, formerly the Queens Hotel now is, all the way to the bottom of Tan Bank, where the Wrekin Buildings and YMCA used to be. Now a new road joins it at the TSB Bank to join Tan Bank higher up.

The name Walker Street has been said to originate with a medieval joke. When fulling cloth the material was put in large tubs with fullers' earth and water; the workers then stamped on the cloth to process it. Those doing this stamping were called 'walkers', though of course they didn't actually get anywhere. However, there may be another explanation.

When I was a boy the most important building in Walker Street was the Public Baths. This was not just a swimming pool but also had 'hip baths' for those who had no bath at home – quite a common problem in the 1920s and 1930s. The water came from a special reservoir in the Limekiln Woods and was changed twice a week, as there was no chlorination plant or circulation. So the water was clean, medium and dirty; charges were 6d for clean, 4d for medium and 2d for dirty water. Men and boys, women and girls, had separate times and days for using the swimming pool and the changing cubicles on the side of the bath. We used to go on Saturdays, swarms of boys, 2d charge for dirty water. At least there was a boiler and it was warm, if somewhat mucky. Don't say that nothing has changed for the better.

Later on, in the 1950s and 1960s as a town councillor, my most important place was the old fire station, at number 14, which was then the council chamber and offices of the Urban District Council. Now it has the Camera Shop of my friend Alan, who also sells fireworks, a restaurant upstairs, a downstairs take-away and the entrance to the market. We councillors met upstairs, 15 of us, and were responsible for the town, roads, water supply, sewerage, 2,000 houses, public loos, parks, gardens, the library, road safety, public health and lots of other things. This form of local government was swept away in 1974, to be replaced by the larger Wrekin District Council, to 'save money'. Readers will not be surprised to find that the new system cost a lot more, and the 'Unitary' council we have now (again to save money) is even more expensive.

Our Civic Society campaigned for ten years and eventually we had a parish council which became Wellington Town Council. Even though it has far fewer powers than the UDC it does stand up for Wellington, which is its function. The Civic Society was formed to campaign for Wellington in 1978 and is still doing that. New members are welcome to this friendly non-party organisation; you don't have to be elected.

Opposite the old UDC offices (market entrance) stands the old library, given to Wellington in 1902 to celebrate the coronation of Edward VII. That part has a pleasant ornamental front and is where the poet Philip Larkin unhappily worked in the 1940s, 'dishing out tripey novels to morons and stoking the stove'. This was extended in the 1960s by the glass-brick part and then the western side, formerly Government offices, previously the Union Brewery and built as the workhouse. Now an excellent new library opened only a couple of years ago stands at the rear. Wouldn't the old library, now disused, make a wonderful museum of The Wrekin?

To the west of the library is the now disused old tax office, sometimes described as the 'lavatorial' building on account of its white (now rather off-white) tiles, which remind many of a public convenience. Since the tax officers moved out it has had many uses; once it was a furniture shop, where goods were displayed and made on the premises, then for a short while it was a Chinese store, which seems to have gone away. Many people, including some councillors, would like to get rid of it.

On the other (east) side of the old library is Edgbaston House, for many years the offices of Gwynne's, the solicitors, coroners etc. This, in the 19th Century, was the office of the Guardians, who operated as local government and the various committees running the workhouse and other parish and town functions. The small white part is the oldest building in Wellington, a medieval house that has been a pub. Behind it leather working was found. Unfortunately it has not been looked after as it should have been and the hand-made ancient bricks have been plastered over. There is an interesting history to this building and I'd advise readers to consult one or more of Allan Frost's books. In fact Allan has published many exceptionally good books on Wellington and I cannot recommend them too highly. While on the subject of history, there's a fascinating amount to be found in the books, magazines and website of Wellington History Group. If you are interested in local history, that's where to start looking.

Like many streets, Walker Street is constantly changing; Lloyds TSB has just returned to being TSB; in 1934 there were Potts, bootmakers and the Mikado Café on the site. The Halifax Building Society is where Walter Davies, the ironmongers had been and the opticians now occupy a building which was once Gwynne and Ross, accountants, shipping agent, and also secretaries to the Wellington and District Chamber of Trade and the Shropshire Omnibus Association Ltd.

There are two Post Offices, neither of which is now operating. The first (east side) was 'too small' so a smaller one replaced it for a few years before the office was moved into the market. Aren't our bureaucrats wonderfully clever?

Wellington, like any town, is constantly evolving. Over the last 90 years I have watched in fascination. There's much more to say but no more space.

BANKING IN WELLINGTON

IN these days of multiple financial crises and bankers being blamed for greed when picking up huge bonuses for making a huge mess of what used to be respectable businesses, perhaps it's time to look back at the origins of banking.

My paternal grandfather, John Evans, farmed at The Ivy House, Weston under Redcastle. He raised beef cattle on his farm, on the Hill estate, Hawkstone. He and his three sons drove the cattle to Wellington to be sold by John Barber. This was before the Great War of 1914 – 1918. His money went into the North and South Wales Bank, which became the Midland and is now the Hong Kong and Shanghai Bank or HSBC.

Grandad introduced his sons to the bank manager when they were 21, as my father did for me, though he had to wait for my return from the Last World War. My other grandfather, Tom Fail, set up a savings account for me when I was born in 1923, so my dealings with the Midland Bank date from 1923 or 1945 if you mean a current account. Not that any of my family has ever had much money of course. Sometimes when we were young there was too much month left at the end of my money and we had an overdraft.

Bank workers, when I remember them first, were all men. They wore black jackets and striped trousers with gold watch chains across their waistcoats, sober ties and starched white collars. There was a huge counter of solid hardwood about six feet wide. Voices were hushed. The Manager (oh yes, he had to have a capital letter) lurked in the background and had a highly polished office somewhere in the rear. It was all very decorous, serious and correct with no need for security grills. Most transactions were in cash – gold, silver and copper.

I looked up a brief history of Wellington's banks in volume XI of the Victoria County History and came up with the following facts:

"At the end of the 18th century there were no regular banking services. In 1805, however, Sir Thomas Eyton, receiver-general for Shropshire and a local landowner formed a banking partnership at Wellington with two local entrepreneurs, John Wilkinson and Richard Reynolds. The bank offered assistance to local industrialists. By 1828 the firm was Reynolds Charlton & Co. with premises in the Market Place. In 1836 the bank united with others in Coalbrookdale, Newport and Shifnal to form the Shropshire Banking Co. (taken over by Lloyds Banking Co. Ltd. in 1874), with a branch in Church Street. Three other banks, eventually incorporated into the clearing banks, opened branches in the town between 1863 and 1926." So that's how our banking system began.

Older readers may remember the Victorian Gothic splendour of Barclays (now unfortunately 'modernised'), the pillared front of Westminster, the brick and stone Lloyds and the Midland with its cupola.

In the 1930s, with its housing boom, the needs of the rising middle classes for mortgages were supplied by several building societies which opened in shops in the town centre. Over the last few years there has been a flurry of mergers and take-overs. An account of mine originally in the Staffordshire passed briefly to a firm whose name I forget and is now with Nationwide. Each time I was rewarded, though not as much as someone in Head Office I'm sure. A smaller staff now has to cope, though modern technology must help. Spectacular take-overs have occurred at the larger Halifax and Trustee Savings Banks, bringing bonuses for a few and problems for many, including the Government.

Now finances seem in flux. Part of this is caused by new technology – credit and debit cards, cash dispensers, phone and internet banking facilities which make transactions much simpler and more convenient for bank customers. Grandad grumbled at the introduction of pound notes. Innovations have, however, meant that original locally based banks are now totally controlled by Head Office and what had been a 'grass-roots' movement became top-down and out of touch. Depleted local staffs struggle to handle larger numbers of customers. My experience is that they do very well despite restrictions and regulations imposed on them.

Some international financial problems have been exacerbated by encouraging customers to get too deeply in debt, selling mortgages to people who could never afford to repay them, governments overspending on public services and sheer incompetence at top levels. Scandals abound. 'Rogue traders', 'casino banking' faulty decision making, near collapses of respected institutions and the mega-bonus culture have led to worldwide protests from many intelligent, responsible people. These protests are in danger of stimulating the 'angry-mob' of violent agitators who make everything much worse.

To return to Wellington and the real life most of us lead, a far cry from all the huge problems we read or hear about. We find the local bank workers, despite tight regulations from 'above' as helpful as they can be. But you can't talk to the manager when they don't have one due to staff cuts.

Taking a pile of cheques, notes and coins from a charity collection, I asked for help to transfer it to the charity concerned. "Sorry, we can't do that." So I asked how it could be done. "Have you the account details of the charity?" No, I said, so let's ring and ask. "We can't do that." Why? "We don't have a telephone." Unusually I was speechless. The local charity shop took the pile and gave me a receipt.

After years of worrying about my bank's lack of ethics, despite over a century of family tradition I've left. The more ethical Co-op Bank has come to Britannia in Market Square and I've joined them. I feel more hopeful. That's about all I can do about the crisis. Thanks to those who have served me well in the past but no thanks to their Head Office who drove me away.

CHAIN OF OFFICE

WELLINGTON UDC'S CHAIRMAN'S CHAIN AND ITS WEARERS

Recently Andrew Eade, then Leader of Telford and Wrekin Borough Council, found in the T&W offices the chain worn by chairmen of Wellington Urban District Council. He thought it should be returned to Wellington and presented it to Wellington Town Council for safe keeping. I thought Wellington News readers would like to know the story of the chain and the men and women who wore it.

Here are my personal memories of the chairmen:

Cecil Lowe, 1950 – 52 together with the clerk, John Broad, initiated the chain and Coat of Arms through the College of Heralds. Cecil was wounded in the Great War, became head of Constitution Hill and Wellington Secondary Modern schools, organised evacuees and wrote local history, mostly for the Shropshire Magazine.

Percy Pearce, 1952 – 53 owned Ercall Garage in Market Street; his understanding of local business was very useful. His firm repaired cars and had a sales showroom where Wilkinson's is now, next to the Wrekin Brewery.

Hugh Herdman, 1953 – 54 was our retired postmaster, a dry wit from Barrow in Furness, who habitually announced exactly how much any proposal would increase the town rates. He used to race Olly Leighton, the treasurer, usually winning until Olly had a calculator.

Alan Hartland, 1954 – 55, perhaps the youngest chairman, was a director of the Victoria Coal and Iron Company, who had the drift mine in Shortwood and a scrap yard in Princes Street. Alan must have been elected soon after he was demobilised.

Graham Murphy, 1955 – 56 and his brother Ronald were sons of OD Murphy who left them Wrekin Brewery, Mineral Water Works and many pubs; Graham was also a Chartered Accountant. They must have been our wealthiest councillors. Feeling broke once I asked Graham how to make money; he replied, "It helps if your father leaves you a brewery".

William Laud, 1956 – 57 ran a shop in Wrekin Road selling sweets, groceries and bread, very popular with children. He had probably retired by the time he was chairman.

Bert Reade 1957 – 58 served in the Royal Flying Corps in the Great War (and a fund of good stories about those days) and had a garage and repair business in Watling Street. One of his best tales was about crawling from a crashed 'kite', with blood all over the place, and being told, "If you didn't have a sense of humour you shouldn't have joined."

Tom Edwards, 1958 – 59 took over Harry Edwards and Sons, undertakers and builders in High Street. He was the eldest of three sons in the trade. Tom was very popular and always 'topped the poll' at elections.

Philip Bott, 1959 – 60 had retired from his job as a railway clerk; he lived in Barnfield Crescent, later in Herbert Avenue. A very short chap, he strongly supported the idea of an abattoir next to the Smithfield Auction.

Ann Jones, 1960 – 61 helped her husband to run Electrical Wholesalers business in Alexandra Road; they lived in Ercall Lane. She had been chairman of the housing committee during a housing boom and was mostly responsible for the building of flats, especially Haughmond Court and Hawkstone Court.

George Evans, 1961 – 62 that's me; you don't need more.

Sidney Parker, 1962 – 63 ran SC Parker & Co, a successful accountancy firm with offices in Bridge Road. He was a valuable chairman of Finance Committee. Sidney and I, with our wives, went to a Buckingham Palace garden party together. In 1963 I left the UDC.

Alan Hartland, 1963 – 64 became chairman again as there were no new candidates with enough committee chairmanship experience to run the council.

Joe O'Connor, 1964 – 65 had a pram and baby equipment shop in Victoria Street. He was the first 'Ratepayers' Association' member to become chairman. This was a new political party set up to protest at the high rates.

Ernie Griffiths, 1965 – 66 was a Civil Servant (a Customs and Excise Officer), lived in Herbert Avenue and later served on Wrekin Council. He had chaired the Ratepayers' Association but when he retired and was allowed to join a political party he joined the Conservative Party. He was also treasurer of the League of Friends of the Princess Royal Hospital.

Tom Edwards, 1966 – 7 served again. Tom always 'topped the poll', a popular man.

John Lovatt 1967 – 68 worked in the distribution of groceries trade and later managed a grocers' shop on the corner of New Street and Market Square. He lived in Crescent Road.

John Bromley, 1968 – 69 ran his family's agricultural implement business in Market Street and Bridge Road.

Ralph Wiseman, 1969 – 70 was a great fund raiser for the Cancer Campaign, extraverted, energetic and determined.

Teddie Morris, 1970 – 71 was a quiet, pleasant man, though I remember little else.

Jean Davidson, 1971 – 72, the first Liberal councillor, was the wife of Dr. Ian, a GP and Police Surgeon. Jean was a leading light in the WVS (later WRVS).

Tom Broadhurst 1972 – 73 Lived in Orleton Lane and had a used car sales business.

Raymond Hall, 1973 – 74 was the last chairman before the abolition of the UDC and formation of Wrekin Council, which he later joined. He saved some of the council's artefacts. Ray lived in Arleston Village and had his own plumbing business. Ray and I are the only two survivors.

While I was on the council there was little concern with party politics except during elections. Only the Ratepayers' Association held group meetings, otherwise there was no block voting. The vice chairman was chosen in an informal meeting of councillors; it was 'Buggins' turn', depending on experience in chairing major committees and automatically voted chairman next year.

For me and, I think, all the others, it felt a great honour to become chairman and wear the chain. We were also automatically appointed magistrates, ex-officio. It was a time of growth and expansion before the decline during Telford's imposition.

03 NEIGHBOURS

MUCH WENLOCK TOWN

Whatever you do, don't call Much Wenlock a sleepy village, because it's not true. There's nothing sleepy about the inhabitants and it's definitely a town, not a village. It's quite a lively little town too and has a lot more than its history on offer, long and exciting as that is.

Much Wenlock is older than England; it was founded long before the English had sorted themselves into a single country. Just how long ago the first settlers came here is not known; it may be several thousands of years before Merewald, king of Mercia gave the land to Milburga for an abbey. Last year the media made a lot about Dr William Penny Brookes starting the modern Olympian Games here (yes, Olympian is the right word) though nobody seems to mention that the first iron bridge was built in Wenlock Borough and is nothing to do with Thomas Telford.

For many centuries Much Wenlock Borough was huge, including a large amount of Wenlock Edge, Ape Dale, Hope Dale and extended northwards over the River Severn, through Madeley to Little Wenlock near The Wrekin. The Borough had its own Member of Parliament, though few people were entitled to vote and a majority could be had for a fee.

Much Wenlock Priory ruins are one of the town's many visitor attractions. It's built of local stone but as the limestone is not friable sandstones have been used for the windows, corners and 'fancy bits'. The rest of the old part of the town is mainly the homes and businesses of artisans and tradesmen. Many have been changed (updated) often through the centuries. One I know well has a 'new' front; added three centuries ago in bricks to the older limestone building behind and some inside walls are lath and plaster.

One of the modern fascinations of the town is its traffic. Wenlockians are about the most polite drivers in the World because the streets are very narrow with lots of parked vehicles and if you aren't going to be polite to other drivers you'll never make it through. It'll take a lot of light flashing, patience and friendly hand waving but all the locals find it simple. It takes a while to understand the code of conduct, especially for 'city slickers'.

There is a brand new secondary school with every possible up to date facility, many of which are shared with the community and is very busy with a multitude of adult activities in the evenings. It's named after Dr Brookes and hosts the Wenlock Olympian Games. These may not be as famous as the International Olympics or as expensive or sophisticated but to my mind they are better because they are far more fun. The fun factor has been almost eliminated in favour of modern 'win at all costs' competitors who become overnight millionaires; nobody gets rich on Wenlock prizes but taking part is enjoyable.

Much Wenlock is a small, historic town populated by 21st Century people.

MEMORIES OF SANKEY'S HADLEY CASTLE WORKS

Here are a few memories of working at Joseph Sankey's works during the Last World War. They are not intended to be anything of a formal history – just personal memories. They may well stimulate others to write in with their own thoughts.

I left school at 16 in 1940 and worked for a time at Allied Ironfounders in Ketley. For this they paid me 12s 6d a week. Then I found from a friend that Sankey's were paying 25s - twice as much - for the same amount of work so quite soon I moved. Who wouldn't?

Apart from wanting some sort of a desk job I had no particular career plan, knowing that I would be 'called up' for war service anyway and the idea of making a career was far from my mind. They sent me to the buying department and told me to share a desk with a chap called Graham. The office was a small partitioned part of the big space where there were many other offices, all glass and steel panels painted and furnished in 'Sankey green', the colour that was everywhere. There were three desks, a large dominating one for the buyer, 'Nick' Nicholson, a smaller one with drawers for his assistant, Mr Delaney and a very plain one for Graham and me.

Graham was a quiet, unassuming sort of chap of about my age who worked very hard and was easy to get on with. Mr Delaney was also quiet and efficient but 'Nick' was a retired Army officer, with a booming voice and a habit of shouting, "Hell's bloody bells!" whenever upset. Many of the other offices had lots of girls in them and they all seemed beautiful and desirable, so at the slightest opportunity I went round to chat them up. The typing pool had so many attractions but their boss was a fierce woman called Dolly, who typed with two fingers but very fast and accurately and she chased me off. Then there was the Hollerith department, where there was a clanging, buzzing rattling version of a computer, the very latest thing for punch cards calculating wages but I couldn't find an excuse to visit that. The records were kept by a filing system operated by girls under the beady eye of Marjorie McCrea who later became a historian.

Lunch was provided at the canteen and was very hierarchical, with rooms for directors, senior staff, staff and a huge place for the people who did the work. We all wore badges, small for the staff and bigger for the workforce. One day a man from the drawing office – I think it was Leslie Frost, Allan's father, explained to me the difference between a mechanic and an engineer. "Look at his top pocket. If there's a spanner he's a mechanic; engineers have a slide rule." These were early calculators. Les talked me into taking a course at Walker Technical College in mechanical engineering, which I attended but failed the second year. Soon afterwards I was called up and that was the end of my plan to become an engineer.

In 1941 almost everyone worked at Sankey's; there were hundreds of bikes and scores of busses bringing workers from all over Shropshire and mid-Wales. I had a bike from Perry's which I parked by the offices. We clocked in and pay was deducted for lateness so I invented a cunning plan enabling me to clock in at 08-29 even though I'd arrived at 08-45. Gradually more work was piled on me and I was ordering steel from Spain and ball bearings from Sweden. How these were delivered I often wondered. One day, after Home Guard all night I fell asleep at my desk. Another time I set the waste paper bin alight with a cigarette end. These were moments of excitement.

Every year there was stocktaking and I discovered the Spitfire shop. Everyone had kept this secret. 'Walls have ears' they said, 'Hitler is listening'. Only recently Allan Frost told me his father was designing amendments to Spitfires and Wellington bombers. The firm was making steel furniture, weapons, armoured carriers and, of course, wheels by the hundreds of thousands. Huge presses from Cincinnati were operated to bend steel sheets. There's a tale of one poor chap who got his head under the press. Some workers were paid by the hour, others were on piecework – the more you did the more you got.

The amount of secrecy was quite wonderful; none of us had much idea what was being manufactured in other parts of the factory, especially when it was munitions or aircraft. Somehow, as I remember, Sankey's had its own peculiar smell, which seemed to be a combination of steel, oil and something else; I remember it still. The noise in some of the shops was deafening.

Harry Hodgson, the Canadian MD, walked round the works every morning saying, "Hi" to everyone. He seemed to know all about each of the thousands of workers and kept his fingers on every pulse in the place. His secretary was Vera Ferriday, an exceptionally bright girl, daughter of a teacher. I rather fancied her but so did lots of us. She used to do the Times crossword while the boss was on his daily perambulations. There was a big poster at Wellington Railway Station advertising 'Sankey's of Wellington' and the telephone number, Wellington Salop 500. There was an efficient telephone exchange, operated by several girls who trilled, "Hello Sankey," when you called.

In many respects, working at Sankey's was quite a happy time – especially compared with the Army. I was busy in the daytime and either Home Guard or Walker Tech or homework in the evenings. Then, in January 1942, came the inevitable letter from the Government with my 'call-up' papers. It was time to end my career as a junior clerk (office boy) and become a soldier. King George wanted me to help him defeat this fellow Hitler.

FOSSILS WITH TALES

Wenlock limestone is famously fossiliferous; it seems the rock consists of little else but fossils. Taking the family (or class) out on a fossil hunt is great fun. Children get quite excited at the idea of chasing fossils, which don't run away so fast that the oldest or youngest members of your group can't catch them.

Many of the houses on the Edge are built of limestone blocks, presumably because they were cheaper and stronger than bricks. Walking through Much Wenlock or any of the villages will make an excellent introduction to a fossil hunt. Why isn't fossil hunting more popular? Perhaps that's because there's no money to be made out of it, so nobody advertises the joys of the chase.

In Ludlow there was once a man called John Norton – a lovely chap with a good way with children and an enormous enthusiasm for palaeontology. He used to head a crocodile of walkers, occasionally picking up a stone, tapping it gently with his hammer and saying, "Hello! Anybody at home?" The rock would break and reveal a fossil, which he would pass round the group. When they had all seen it, he'd add, "You are the first humans to see this little chap, because he died long before our sort of animal was invented."

John was the volunteer custodian of Ludlow museum, where there were cases full of fossils brought in by children. Each exhibit was carefully named (Latin of course) and had the name of the child or adult who had donated it.

When taking a youth group to a hunt, a man-sized lad asked me the name of a fossil he'd found. I suggested he asked a nearby tiny girl, who said, "It's a pentamerus oblongus but I've got a better one at home". What a put-down!

Hang on! There's something I should have said; we don't want to get into trouble do we? The fossils belong to whoever owns the land, or wall or house they are in. So it is important to make sure you have the necessary permission. Have a word with the locals, especially local geologists, to find out where it is safe and legal to take them. Also, there are books and maps about the best places to go and what you might find there. Beware, palaeontology can be addictive.

Here's wishing you and all your friends happy hunting.

CRAVEN ARMS
GUARDIAN OF WENLOCK EDGE

The small town of Craven Arms sits in a junction of river valleys guarding the south end of Wenlock Edge. Although I knew it well when I was teaching there from 1947 to 1949 there have only been short occasional visits since then. Perhaps someone might like to bring this brief description up to date; I'd like to know about its modern development.

The school's headmaster was Mr Davies; I never discovered his first name, but behind his back he was called 'Ducky'. He said, "I'll try you out for a month and if I like you, you can stay. If not you'll have to find somewhere else." He handed me a class of 50 lads, saying, "Teach them scripture. They've all got bibles. Here's a stick, use it if you like but don't mark the register, that's a job for a proper teacher." He then walked out. Having no idea what to do, I seized on Psalm 23 and we chanted that for an hour. He decided to keep me.

He was a kind man but could be terrifying when he wished to be. Local girls told me they knew when they had grown up; that's when 'Ducky' raised his hat to them in the street.

'The Arms', as it's sometimes called, is mainly a railway settlement at a junction of several routes, though some smaller places like Stokesay and Halford are very much older. There have been changes and expansion since I was there. It was the subject of a dissertation I wrote for London University, based on its historical geography and sketching the effects of the underlying physical structure of the area, human settlement evolution and technological developments on its growth from semi-isolated settlements to a communications hub.

This is where several of 'the valleys of springs of rivers', as Housman put it, meet; consequently it is a meeting place of routes. Not only do valley routes meet here but also prehistoric ridgeways. The geology is varied and interesting enough to attract students and palaeontologists. One spot we called the 'Onny Section' had its own trilobite named after a local postman, Jim Hughes, who found it, though when I asked at the appropriate museum to see one I was met with blank incomprehension.

There is a good deal of evidence of prehistoric settlement around here, though I know little of its investigation. The terrain was surely quite suitable for farming, hunting and gathering, especially during the Bronze and Iron Ages. An important Roman road passes through, going from Castra Deva (Chester) in the north to Bravonium (Leintwardine) in the south and there is a well-defined marching camp on Norton's Camp.

Stokesay Castle is actually a fortified manor house and a very fine example too. The site, I was told, was chosen by a Norman and its position on low land instead of available, easily defended hill sites, puzzled me a little until discovering that he was a cavalryman. Most of the building seems to have been by a Ludlow wool merchant. The 'castle' and the nearby church figured in the Civil War, though accounts suggest that the Parliamentarians simply frightened the Royalists who held it into submission.

When the Railway Age came, this place found itself on an important main line, with junctions through Mid-Wales in the west and through Much Wenlock to Wellington in the north-east. Local farming interests seized on this opportunity and several agricultural developments began to be built, especially a once thriving stock market. In the 1940s the annual sheep sale was huge and internationally acclaimed with over 50,000 sheep sold for export to Australia, New Zealand, Argentina, Canada and the USA.

For the last few months of my visit I was sent to Wistanstow, a little way north, to teach there as the headmaster, Harold Tarver, was ill. That too was a lovely school and well run. On my first day there I was sitting with a class, wondering what to do, when suddenly, without warning, the whole class sprang to attention. The vicar had just walked in behind me! We went out a few times on 'nature study' expeditions and all enjoyed them.

My memories of Craven Arms between 1947 and 1949 are all happy ones. During the weekdays I lived with Margaret Jones ('Auntie Mag') at Millbro, Corvedale Road and went home to Wellington each weekend. Evenings were in 'The Bottom' (Stokesay Castle Hotel) or more often studying geography and education or walking with Jim Hughes, an enthusiastic amateur geologist. Jim had an encyclopaedic knowledge of the area which came in very useful for my dissertation.

Since those days I have visited occasionally and noticed changes, some but not all for the better. Hall Warteridge and Owen had a big livestock auction; has it gone? The rather magnificent post office is no more. The school is now a primary, though it had children from 5 to 14; the leaving age became 15 while I was there. Do the older ones now go to Church Stretton or Ludlow? There are new museums, so presumably there's now a tourist trade, which I hope prospers. The A49 is even more busy. My dissertation map showed a proposed by-pass to the east of the town; information I had gathered from the Shropshire County Council's planning department. However, that seems not to have happened.

How fares Craven Arms now?

"Here's a stick, use it if you like but don't mark the register, that's a job for a proper teacher"

ADMASTON IN THE EARLY 1930s

Many years ago, in about 1930 or 1931, when I was seven or eight, we moved house to Admaston, so I was sent to school in Wrockwardine. We lived on the corner of what we called 'Cowmuck Lane' but may have officially been Smithy Lane, now called Elmsdale Crescent. We gave it the cowmuck name because a herd of cattle were driven twice a day from the fields now full of houses to the south of Station Road down to Admaston Hall Farm to be milked. They certainly left their mark.

Our house was called Melbourne; it's still there though most people don't use house names any more. We paid 15 shillings a week rent to Mr. Turner of Admaston Hall; he paid the rates. It's semi-detached; there were three bedrooms and a 'box room' upstairs, a living room, sitting room (kept for best and not often used because of the trouble and expense of laying the fire) and a scullery, with a lavatory and coal house outside. There was no bathroom but at least the lavatory was a flush WC instead of the earth closet we had, had before.

The house had its own well, under the living room floor, probably just a thin tube, and water had to be pumped up to a big tank in the roof, from where it supplied pipes and two taps in the scullery. It was my job to pump the water up, using a 'semi-rotary' pump with a large handle that went backwards and forwards. You could hear the water splashing into the tank, which I usually filled on Sunday nights ready for washday Monday. There was no hot water supply except from kettles on the fire.

We used a tin bath in front of the fire, filled from kettles. Washing was in the sink. Clothes were washed in a big bowl in the scullery, which had a fireplace underneath. There was a radio with valves and wet and dry batteries, attached to a long aerial outside. Cooking was on the Triplex range with two ovens around which hot air from the fire could be diverted by dampers. Boiling, frying and toasting were done over the fire, though not all at once. There was electric lighting but no wall sockets or gas. Deliveries were regular, including bread from Frosts, coal, milk, potatoes, vegetables, fish and ice cream from Tranquillo Sidoli; most were by horse. Scissor grinders, onion sellers and the rag-and-bone came occasionally.

There was almost no garden to the house, which was a great change from our previous place where there must have been about an acre. Consequently we had to buy potatoes and vegetables that had always been home grown. There were a few flowers in the front and some soft fruit bushes at the side. A small shed housed the garden tools and my 'chemistry set' containing a few test tubes with powdered, liquid and crystalline chemicals, mostly now unobtainable from a chemist shop and illegal to possess.

Unlike most people in Admaston my father had a car. He needed it when he had a job or to find a job when he was unemployed. This he kept down at the smithy in a garage that used to be the smith's workshop for shoeing horses. If (or rather when) anything went wrong he had to mend it himself because he couldn't afford to pay anyone else. Dad worked at several jobs, often at the same time. He sold paint to places like the sugar beet factory and some scale-prevention gadgets called Scale Buoys that saved industrial boilers from filling with furred up deposits of lime from the local hard water. These looked like large electric light bulbs and contained an inert gas and a blob of mercury that glowed in the dark when it was moved; I haven't seen any since the Last

World War, perhaps because they were made by a German company. He was also an agent for the Commercial Union. Once he bought the materials to manufacture batteries in the shed but this was not a success as he couldn't sell them, unsurprisingly because they looked very rough and amateur. None of these things brought in much money and he had to give up his car and take a job at Lane's agricultural tool works in Queen Street, Wellington and go on a bike.

Sundays were extremely boring. First was Sunday School at the Methodist Chapel, smelling of musty bibles. Well meaning old men and middle aged women read passages from the Bible and convinced themselves they were doing us good. The worst were the Old Testament stories and miracles because I was old enough to question their veracity but not old enough to keep quiet about it. In the evenings we went to St. Peter's church in Wrockwardine.

I was given a football – a proper case-ball with a leather cover and a rubber bladder. We didn't have proper teams, just kicked the ball about off Ringer's Lane until one of the boys broke it beyond repair. I had an iron hoop made by the blacksmith with a wire handle looped round it for better control and a catapult with strong elastic and a leather sling. We did a bit of bird spotting, especially at the local sewage works and egg collecting (never more than one from a nest) and I remember still seeing my first kingfisher.

Each week I read Comic Cuts and swapped it for Rover, Hotspur and any other boys' magazine I could get. I read all the books in the house and everything available including the Daily Mail, Christian Herald but especially the Children's Encyclopaedia – ten volumes, thousands of pages and illustrations of everything Arthur Mee thought was good for young boys to know about. In fact Arthur Mee was my best teacher.

That's a short summary of life between 1930 and 1935 as I remember it. They say the past is a different country; that's very true.

"We used a tin bath in front of the fire, filled from kettles. Washing was in the sink. Clothes were washed in a big bowl in the scullery, which had a fireplace underneath"

04 THE WREKIN

THE ERCALL WOODS

Which is the second highest hill in The Wrekin forest? Most local people would answer, "The Ercall" and be wrong, because Maddocks Hill, south of the Ercall is actually higher, despite the huge amount of rock extracted from it, though not so well known. However, the Ercall certainly seems to be the second hill of The Wrekin range, especially when seen from Wellington or anywhere else to the north.

Most us think of Ercall woods as the area between Ercall Lane and Wrekin Golf Course, bounded in the west by the Forest Glen road and in the south east by the M54. That is the area I am writing about. It includes the Ercall hill and also the smaller Lawrence hill to the west of the Ercall. Nearly all this area is wooded, much of it ancient coppice oak but some is much more recent, the resurgent forest that has replaced quarrying.

The woods to the north of the Ercall ridge are owned by T&W Borough council, inherited from Wellington UDC and Shropshire CC, except for a small patch opposite Buckatree Hall Hotel, which is the hotel's property. The rest, including Lawrence Hill, was bought by the Shropshire Wildlife Trust from Lord Forester with a lot of local help a few years ago.

There was great consternation in the 1980s when Lord Forester, who owned most of the wood, proposed building holiday chalets in the quarries which were just beginning to recover from the extraction of millions of tonnes of rock to provide hardcore for Telford's roads and buildings. The plans were greatly disapproved, especially by local dog walkers, of whom there are many. Eventually, after much argument and protest the council rejected them.

Although the woods seem to be wild apart from many pathways and quarries there is a long history of use of the rocks. There seem to be traces of the beautiful pink Granophyre that is sometimes called Ercallite in the surfacing of the Roman Watling Street and also in Thomas Telford's reconstruction as Holyhead Road. Both appear to have used Granophyre chippings as a top dressing and these were extensively used for gravel drives in big houses – Apley, Orleton, Dothill and Sunnycroft among others – in Victorian times. It was then referred to as Ercall Gravel.

The much softer Tuff rock, a mixture of volcanic ash and lava, is at the east end of the hill and is cut through by the M54. This rock was designated as too soft to provide hardcore for the motorway; though I have been told it was in fact used for some of the roadway embankments, surreptitiously. Trucks carried off the rock excavated from the cutting, turned at a road island and returned to deposit it for the embankment. So I am told. Tuff was also sold years ago as a cheaper substitute for Granophyre.

The other main rock to be found in the area is Wrekin Quartzite; this has been the target of the huge quarries on the Ercall and Lawrence hills for the construction of Telford New Town's superstructure. The enormous destruction of the hills, the vegetation and wildlife is the price this beautiful landscape has had to pay for the construction of Telford. Was it worth it?

During operations the quarry workers discovered traces of gold in the quartzite. Excitedly they examined it and wondered if it was in economic quantities. To their intense disappointment they found, after some calculation, that the cost of refining the gold was more than the price for it at local jewellers' shops. There are also iron deposits and at one point is an 'ochre spring', where rusty red water emerges to join the brook through the Ercall/Lawrence quarries that empties into the

Buckatree pool.

In a few places there are deposits of Rhyolite, Lower Comley Sandstone and the fossiliferous Shineton shale. The particular interests of geologists, however, are the unconformities between Cambrian and Precambrian rocks and wave marks in the Quartzite. This is a very complex and interesting area and is frequently visited by students of geology, confirmed by its designation as a Site of Special Scientific Interest (SSSI). Some of the vegetation is regularly cleared so that the rock formations can be examined.

One of the important early explorers of the area was Charles Callaway, a Doctor of Science in Geology who investigated this and other places in 19th Century and wrote about it. He taught at Hiatt's Ladies College and was buried in our local cemetery. Dr Calloway's life and times have been studied by Wendy Palin, Wellington History Group's Treasurer; I hope she will write about him some time for Wellingtonia.

The Wildlife Trust and their volunteers work hard to preserve and protect the vegetation and creatures of the woods. To some of us the most fascinating aspect of the whole area is the way Nature has fought back and the natural forest has been recolonising the quarries, gradually turning the 'moonscape' back to its natural beauty. Resurgence of Nature is a quite wonderful yet little appreciated occurrence. Unfortunately the term 'scrub' is too often ascribed to it, suggesting waste land. It is really 'baby forest' and will develop anywhere, especially in our gardens, where it can be a delight or a pain depending on our attitude to wildlife.

These woods are quite unique and some of the most diverse and complex places on Earth. Although used frequently by local walkers they are insufficiently appreciated.

A FOREST SCHOOL AT SHORTWOOD

How old is Short Wood School? It depends what you mean by a school. Surely children and teachers are what matters. This building is very young but the tradition is ancient. Short Wood is really Ercall Junior and Barn Farm schools, which came from the old Prince's Street; the schools moved but the buildings stayed or were demolished. This 'new' school is really in its third century.

My family's connections with Prince's Street (that's the proper way to spell it) began when my mother started there, aged five, in 1893 and paid two pence a week to go. It was the Wesleyan Methodist School.

Naomi Hurdley went there in 1933 until passing the 'scholarship' for the Girls' High in 1944. T. Cliff Buttrey was Headmaster even then. She married me in 1950 and our sons Paul and Mark attended in 1959 – 1964 and 1963 – 1968, both going to Orleton Park.

In 1953 I moved to Prince's Street, working there until 1964. It was mostly a very enjoyable time; for Cliff let us try our ideas. My best was Lookout Club, an excuse for taking children out of school for walks in the woods and round town. We dipped ponds, climbed trees and rocks, collected wild flowers, grasses and fungi. We learned map reading, surveying, and lots of other things. I'd get the sack for it now because of Health and Safety laws but we all had a lot of fun.

This is the tradition I hope will be continued with Forest School.
Two warnings for the teachers:
1. This is so enjoyable you'll find yourself working extra hard and long hours.
2. Many years later you'll be accosted by ex-pupils you have inspired.
My very best wishes to Forest School. May it flourish and HAVE FUN.

BACKWOODS OF THE WREKIN FOREST - LIMEKILN WOOD

Many parts of The Wrekin Forest have few visitors. This is very good for wildlife but I often think that a lot of walkers who are keen naturalists are missing out. Most visitors to The Wrekin simply walk up the main path I call the Pilgrims' Way to the top, look at the vast panorama of the view and come down again, perhaps pausing for refreshments at Halfway House. That's fine and most enjoyable but there are other woods in the forest where hardly anyone goes.

Most of the animals, birds, insects and plants whose homes are in these quiet, secluded woods would be horrified if the many joggers and bikers who think of The Wrekin as a 'Green Gym', simply a good place to take their exercise and keep fit, invaded their territory. Wild creatures prefer to stay wild. They would also be unhappy to meet some of the uncontrolled and excitable dogs that race around the main paths.

South-east of The Wrekin are the Ercall and Lawrence hills, of which I have written previously in Wellingtonia. South of the Ercall Wood is Wrekin Golf Course and south-east of that is Limekiln Wood, a fascinatingly varied collection of geology and wildlife habitats.

If you walk in here, do be very careful to keep to the paths, whether they are official rights of way or those used by others. There have been, over several centuries, mines and pits opened up to access the minerals lying beneath the woods. These pits are dangerous and great care is needed, especially when leaves are on the trees, as most of them have been filled with assorted vegetation and they occur at irregular intervals. You could fall down a pit and not be seen for a long time, perhaps too long. Keep to human paths; some of the tracks are made by other animals that may be far shorter than you and perhaps just looking for grass or worms. Please don't frighten the creatures, tread on the plants or get yourself hurt.

One access to Limekiln Wood is from Golf Links Lane. There's a space for parking where the tarmac veers right to the golf club's car park. An ancient Holloway heads south, crossing the golf links near the site of 'the Dormie House' to join the Hatch farm track. Left (east) a footpath takes you to the old reservoirs that used to supply Wellington. These pools are sometimes fished. Princes Street School used them for pond dipping in the 1950s and 1960s; great fun and much learning.

Further on are the old lime kilns, where the carboniferous limestone from under the wood was burned to produce quicklime, slaked with water to produce slaked lime. The kilns are worth the trouble of finding among rampant vegetation. Slaked lime was used for enhancing crop growth on farms; other limestone was for flux in the iron furnaces. Iron ore, coal and lime were placed in the furnaces and the coal ignited. Air was blown into the furnace and the iron melted. Lime mixed with impurities in the ore, separating them from the molten iron, which could then be poured into moulds.

Near the kilns are the few remaining houses of the hamlet of Steeraway, once a very busy place, with extensive quarries and mines in the narrow strip of limestone stretching south-east from the kilns. Most of the mines have been capped and closed but there's one adit that is still open to those brave (or foolhardy) enough to enter. There are gaping holes in the tops of the kilns which are very dangerous. Children worked in the mines and quarries until a damning report of their dreadful conditions was published by mine inspectors; that virtually closed the whole complex.

To read a much fuller report of the old hamlet of Steeraway, find an article by Wellington History Group's chairman, Neil Clarke. He has researched the extensive coal and lime workings in the area and the network of transport, including jinny rails that delivered the processed lime to farms and factories. It's currently out of print but he might be able to organise a reprint; otherwise there's a copy in Wellington Library.

Going south from Steeraway is a track to the Hatch Farm, roughly parallel to a footpath in the middle of the wood and the old Hollybush Lane, now usually called Golf Links Lane. The limekilns are on your right and a footpath takes you through Steeraway farm to Short Wood. Further on, the stony track goes between Limekiln Wood and Black Hayes, with an adit under the track, a very spooky place. Further still, just before the track comes to fields on the right is the site of the old Gamekeeper's cottage, opposite which is an older house site, the scene of a novel by Hesba Stretton and in my mother's time the home of a poor old woman she called 'Old Annie' and her many children.

Now back to the old reservoirs. Through the middle of the wood is s footpath designated as the Hutchinson Way until it reaches the limit of T&W Borough ownership, turns right and joins the main track. Well hidden within the wood was once the home of a recluse we called Jungle Jim, now demolished. 'Jim' reportedly met a sticky end. I found him a friendly chap, though he had a big chip on his shoulder.

If, instead of turning right to follow Hutchinson Way you keep straight on it's a lovely walk along the sandstone woodlands to the fields at the top of Maddocks Hill, with narrow paths; straight on through the huge Camptonite quarry or right to join the lane to the Hatch. This area is privately owned but there are no 'Keep Out' notices and the paths are clearly well used.

To really understand this woodland takes many visits, searching for variations of geology, plantlife and archaeological/historical sites. I have taken years and only know a little.

"Most visitors to The Wrekin simply walk up the main path I call the Pilgrims' Way to the top, look at the vast panorama of the view and come down again"

A WALK IN THE WOOD

HOW TO ENJOY THE WREKIN FOREST

Some time ago I was invited to talk to some young teachers on a course designed to equip them for taking classes of children into the woods as part of their education. I felt I had to warn them of the consequences. First there is a danger that you will be so thrilled with the children's enthusiasm that you will find yourself working with them out of school hours for no pay. Second you will find that over the years they will come up to you in the street to thank you for inspiring them. That's if you do it right.

Nowadays it's much more difficult. The dreaded 'Elf and Safety' laws forbid anyone to do anything that might, or just possibly could, be a threat to the kids. The rules seem too often like 'Whatever you do, don't'. We went pond dipping, tree climbing and so on, just a class or group of 30 or 40 youngsters and me. We did that for years without any casualties except for one poor lad who walked into a lamp post. The only rule imposed was 'In Loco Parentis', meaning I should treat children as a good parent would treat their own children. That's fair enough and anyway sometimes one of them was mine. I do hope someone in authority will change the regulations to something more sensible. All that's needed is for the teacher to take full responsibility for the wellbeing of his/her class.

Most people seem to think that a walk on The Wrekin is just up to the top and back. That's fine for those who like it but there's a lot more to The Wrekin Forest than the magnificent views from the top and the prehistoric hillfort. Wandering through the Ercall quarries, spotting the array of rocks and the wonderful way in which nature has fought back from the disaster of tearing the woods apart to provide rubble to build Telford. Just to see the way so much wild vegetation and animals have recolonised what I remember as a moonscape of rock is a joy. Just stand there and marvel.

Limekiln Wood is an education in itself. There are the kilns themselves, an old well, caverns, traces of ancient lime working to wonder about, fossils in the limestone, orchids, badger setts... There's so much to see it can take weeks. Also some of these woods are on sandstone, where the vegetation is subtly different.

Maddocks Hill has had its core bulldozed away for Telford's roads by the corporate vandals, but this has exposed some fascinating rocks and again the forest is fighting back hard; soon the deep gash where millions of tonnes of rock have been gouged away will be semi-mature forest. The indigenous vegetation is going great guns and is well on the way to becoming much the same mixed forest that was cruelly killed by the quarrying.

Black Hayes (did you know there was such a place?) is part of the 'back woods' that are hardly ever visited. It's pocked with coal pits and pit mounds, many of which are dangerous, especially in summer and autumn when the trees are in full leaf. There's a place called the badgers' coal mine, where a sett has been long established.

The Little Hill woods at the southwest end of The Wrekin are all planted, mostly with conifers, though the plans are changing and many parts are now interspersed with broadleaf. These make a change of scene from the more natural forest. South of The Wrekin are Gibbons Coppice and Wenlocks Wood, where worrying changes of ownership and style are taking place. They're not walker-friendly like the woods owned by the Orleton and Raby estates, the Shropshire Wildlife Trust and the Borough Council.

Short Wood and Spring Coppice are at the east end of the forest and are under serious threat from opencast coalmining. There have been many public inquiries which have persuaded the authorities not to permit the desecration of this beautiful place but the last one was heavily balanced against the locals, ignoring all evidence against it. So permission was given to rip up the forest, pollute the atmosphere, annoy the inhabitants and destroy the wonderful ambience.

Fortunately all is not yet lost. A number of brave enthusiasts are camping in the wood and they have a network of tunnels and shafts as well as friends who are willing to come to their aid when needed. They are intelligent and determined and some of our laws are on their side. It will take a lot of effort and cost a lot of money to move them. They know that they have right on their side. This small area of outstanding natural beauty is vital to the physical and mental health of the people of its environment as well as the wildlife in and around its boundaries. It should be held sacred, not sacrificed to feed a polluting power station for a short while.

Wellington is The Wrekin's own market town, anciently called 'Wellington under The Wrekin' and the best base for visits, as well as the hometown of 'All Friends Round The Wrekin'. Many Wellingtonians walk regularly in the forest, either solo or with their friends, children and dogs. There's free parking, plenty of assorted food and drink, a large, excellent market (open Tuesday, Thursday, Friday and Saturday), swimming pool and leisure centre, as well as accommodation.

Here The Wrekin and its forest are much loved and often thought of as a sacred mountain, a place of devotion, the symbol of the lands and people of this area. It is full of secret places, of traces of history, archaeology, geology, biology; of the passage of the seasons and the weather. A thorough search for its wonders can take a lifetime of wandering in the woods.

Apart from all this, the exercise of walking and looking is good for your body as well as for your mind.

"Just to see the way so much wild vegetation and animals have recolonised what I remember as a moonscape of rock is a joy. Just stand there and marvel"

05 CHANGES

RANDOM MEMORIES OF MY SCHOOLDAYS

When I was three and a bit my parents sent me off to school. Why so early? I've no idea except perhaps that I chattered too much. Betty and Mary Greenfield took me up Constitution Hill to the infants' school opposite the Union Free Church. I remember very little except the high ceiling, half-tiled walls and a lady called, 'Miss', who bossed us all about. The others were learning the alphabet and had got as far as V for vase, with its picture on the classroom wall. All the other letters had their pictures too; apple, ball, cup and so on. Miss was pleased that I had already learned the other letters but less pleased that I wanted to go on to the little letters; a b c d e... because I didn't know all of them. She had to teach the capitals W X Y Z before starting on the little letters and I would have to wait.

How long I was there I don't know but we moved house and I was sent to another school in the country, about two miles walk from home. They wouldn't have me because I wasn't five so I would have to wait over a year. While waiting I had to have an operation to remove my tonsils. This was a horrible experience, especially as they didn't give me enough chloroform and I was conscious while the lump of flesh was cut from my throat. Then I had bovine TB, the cure for which involved Dad sticking a probe into my neck night and morning for nine months. School was put off again. I read all the books and magazines and newspapers in the house while I was waiting to get back to school.

At last they let me go to school. Oddly I remember little except the earth playground and the corrugated iron frame round the boys' urinal. There's just a little memory of the very high windows in the classrooms, presumably so that we couldn't look at anything outside and be distracted from our lessons. There was some surprise that I was able to keep up with the others except that I didn't know anything of the Catechism, which was important in the Church of England school. That's what they all taught, Reading, Writing, Arithmetic, Scripture and a bit of 'Physical Training' if it wasn't raining.

My third and last primary school was Wrockwardine Boys' School, when we had moved to live in Admaston. This I remember quite well. It wasn't the one by the church – that was for infants and girls; babbies and wenches as we used to say. It was on the right of the Avenue, later to become a shop. The headmaster's house was at the far end and there were two classrooms and a cloakroom. The land around it had the head's garden by his house and the rest was a little playground for the lads, surrounded by a high wall. There's still the word BOYS carved in the stone lintel above one of the doors.

Again the curriculum was reading, writing, arithmetic and scripture. We read mostly old, tatty books, and copied from the blackboard writing like this:

A B C D E   The quick brown fox jumps over the lazy dog

If it wasn't exactly like Billy Mainwaring's writing you 'got the stick'. He was good at it and so were we.

Arithmetic was mostly tables, especially 16 ozs = 1 lb, 14 lbs = 1 stone, 28 lbs = 2 stones =

1 quarter, 4 quarters = 56lbs = 1cwt, 20 cwt = 1 ton. Money had £, s, d, plus halfpennies and farthings. Farthings were not so small amounts as we could spend them on sweets like gob-stoppers and liquorish boot-laces. Lengths were in inches, feet, yards, chains, furlongs and miles. One already out of date measurement I remember was 5 ½ yards = 1 rod, perch or pole.

Billy Mainwaring (pronounced Mannering) was the Headmaster and taught the 11 to 14 boys, while young Sammy Parker had the 7 to10s. The leaving age was 14, though some left early if they got a job. It was thoroughly boring and could be brutal but nobody left without being able to read, write, do sums and know their catechism. Illiteracy was thoroughly beaten out of us. There were no secretaries or helpers, no playground supervisors, no paranoid fences or locks. Most of the lads grew up and had happy lives.

We played hide and seek at dinner time after we'd wolfed our butties. We charged round the village playing fox and hounds, usually landing up on Gorsey Bank, or 'Gossy Bonk'. We kicked tin cans when we didn't have a ball, mostly because nobody could afford one. We made tops and whipped them, made hoops and sticks, made catapults and missed hundreds of birds; I don't remember anyone actually hitting anything he aimed at. We played Tin Can Murky a lot. The marbles season came after conkers, when there were muddy puddles everywhere. One lad taught me to make a flute.

Some games were a bit rough – well more than a bit. But usually the older boys were kind to the little 'uns. Schoolboy ethics said it was OK to hit anyone bigger than yourself or any smaller kid if he was cheeky or hit you first. Wrockwardine had another rule – Barlies. If you were not playing a game as it rushed past you only had to shout, 'Barlies' to be left alone.

Most of the lads were countrymen, who knew where all the birds were nesting, how to blow eggs and never ever took more than one egg from a nest or disturbed the birds. They could find where rabbits ran and catch them with wire snares, find huge mushrooms for breakfast and milk a cow into a jug. Some regularly took one of Major Herbert's pheasants but most didn't dare.

Was life better or worse then?

RUBBER DUCKS MADE IN WELLINGTON

In the early 1950s the Chad Valley Toy Company had a factory in Orleton Lane, Wellington for the manufacture of various rubber toys. Because they were made of latex, which has perished and disintegrated over the years there are few, if any of them still around.

By far the best selling product was a rubber duck, which was popular for floating in the bath. They don't seem to be around any more, probably because most of us now prefer to have a shower.

As my father was, for a while a sort of foreman there I was able to see the way they were made, which might be of interest to Wellingtonia readers.

The first one made was either of wood or clay – wood I think – and that served as a model for the rest. This was put in a container and plaster of paris poured in half way up. When that set the top half of the mould was made which was separated into two halves and a groove made for pouring in the liquid latex which had some sort of oil mixed with it to keep it from prematurely setting. This was then put into an electric oven and baked for a short time, after which some of the latex was poured away from the inside, leaving it hollow. It then went back into the oven and was baked again for a few more minutes.

After cooling the two halves of the mould were separated and the rubber models passed on to the trimmers, stuffers, painters and packers. Surplus rubber was cut off, the inside was stuffed with kapok and sealed either with waterproofing or a squeaker and finally paint was added.. The moulds were used many times.

After this they were individually boxed and packed by dozens, which were packed into grosses, and in turn into great grosses (12 X 12 =144 [gross] and 144 X 12 = 1728 [great gross]). Why this old fashioned system was used I never knew; nor did my father.

As well as rubber ducks Flook was produced (see earlier Wellingtonia). There were other products including, as my son remembered, a rubber monkey. Most of the workforce were local women and girls. It was a smelly job with all the latex and Heaven knows what 'Elfansafety' would think nowadays but they seemed a happy, cheerful crew.

JOHN CRUMP BOWRING AND 'THE REC'

As I'm writing this I have just returned from a stroll in what we used to call 'The Rec.' but now seems officially known as Bowring Park. I asked several people what they called it and it seems that those who have been here a long time talk about The Rec, short for recreation ground and the younger folk call it a park. Now seems a good time to write about it and the man who gave it (or rather part of it) to Wellington.

John Crump Bowring was a fishmonger. According to the story I was told many years ago he came to Wellington from Grimsby, just after the new railway enabled fast transport around the country. I'm told he brought a box of fresh fish to the market; they sold out very quickly because local people had never had access to fresh sea fish before. He was delighted and came next week with two boxes, which he sold quickly and the week after he brought four boxes.

I wonder how he got the middle name 'Crump'. Perhaps the same way William Penny Brookes acquired his. It presumably sounded more middle-class than an ordinary common Christian name. Anyway, JCB was a good friend of Wellington.

Soon he was becoming rich. He opened a shop, then a bigger one, then another and another, and began to trade as a wholesaler as well. He built himself a big house – Bradley Moor in Haygate Road - and bought the land across the road.

John Crump Bowring gave the cast iron gates to All Saints church and the railings where the old town gaol or lock-up used to be. His widow gave the Cottage Hospital.

Bowring gave the land opposite his house to 'The people of Wellington' for a recreation ground on condition that brass bands should never play there. I suppose he just didn't want to hear brass band music from his home; I don't think there has ever been one. It was not given to the council but to the people of Wellington. I was once a Trustee; I wonder who the trustees are now?

My first memories of 'The Rec' were before the Last World War, when we lived at Orleton Cottage, opposite where the cricket pitch is now. Two things from that time are gone; there was an ancient army tank that was taken for scrap during the War and the oldest of the copper beech trees. In the 1950s that was in danger of dying and everyone loved it, so two new ones were planted, one each side. There are more now, ready to take over.

In its early days the Bowring Recreation Ground was a very popular venue for us Wellingtonians, as it is now. There were a lot more bedding plants and less playing equipment. The Rec extended then southwards about as far as the last tennis court. It was not until the late 1950s and early 1960s that it was extended.

Wellington Urban District Councillors were always proud of the Bowring and until they were abolished in 1974 they looked after it carefully. In the 1950s the Council bought land to the south, including access to Holyhead Road.

The UDC bought some fields from the Carver family and the then Engineer and Surveyor, Arthur Barton, set about designing the rest of the park. We thought it was a very clever idea to have two football pitches with a cricket square between them so that the football pitches could be used in the season and during the summer and serve as the outfield for cricket. I have been told that there is some argument currently about the precise dimensions of the soccer pitch on the south side and some official is saying it can't be used for competition matches. That would be a great pity.

Changing rooms were also provided at this stage and these seem to be still well used. This included the small car park and the entrance from Herbert Avenue, which was quite adequate in the 1950s but now seems much too small, leading to parking in the Avenue when matches are on. If readers worry about the rather wiggly path from Holyhead Road they should blame me. I suggested that the straight path Arthur Barton had planned would be more interesting if it had a wiggle or two in it.

At the same time the UDC provided a paddling pool, complete with shelter and water purification plant. This was very popular with youngsters for many years until some 'yobs' decided it would be fun to break glass in it. Eventually it had to be emptied and cleaned too many times and finally it was demolished.

Last time I looked there were dog walkers, teenagers kicking a ball, teens and adults playing tennis, children enthusiastically at play, adults (some almost my age) playing bowls, a couple of joggers, teenagers just sitting chatting, mums and dads watching their kids, disabled people being pushed around and folks just enjoying the sunshine. That was when there were no matches on, no spectators and not at a time when Lions on and off Wheels were attracting huge numbers to their excellent event.

The recent refurbishment by Telford and Wrekin Borough Council has been a great boon to everyone. My congratulations go to the councillors who provided the public money and who, with council officials, liaised with Wellington Town Council and very many neighbours and users. I was amazed and delighted when Becky Eade asked about the history of the site. A really good job has been done on The Rec, as witnessed by all the many people who come from around Wellington and district to enjoy its many facilities.

There were dark days when it was called 'The Wreck' and had been sadly neglected for several years. If it's now called Bowring Park, that's fine; it's an asset to our town and, just for once, public money well and wisely spent.

HIGH STREET WELLINGTON HAS CHANGED

On Midsummer Day, 1923, there was an addition to the Evans family who lived over their furniture shop at 49 High Street, Wellington, Salop. They had, according to reports by neighbours, a fat baby. A while later they took him over to the Methodist Church down the road and had him christened George Thomas. They used to leave him in his pram, outside the shop, with their dog, Rex, guarding him. When asked if he had only one child, his father replied, "One's quite enough".

Since then High Street has changed a lot and I've been watching the changes happen. Today I took my camera for a walk up and down the street and was absolutely amazed by the differences, not only from the 1920s but also from the time we lived there in 1952, in a flat above two shops.

Almost everything seems altered now. In the 1920s High Street was more or less respectable on the front, mainly small houses, pubs and shops, with some pretty dreadful slums and grinding poverty behind. Places like Chapel Lane, Parton Square and New Square ('Little Ireland') were notorious for squalor, drunken fights and police only going in fours.

In the 1950s things were changing. The worst slums had been demolished and the people were housed in the hundreds of new council houses that were built in Regent Street, Ercall Gardens, Urban Gardens, Hollies Road etc. This was making a great improvement in the lives of many people, who often had their first bathroom and lavatory.

Loss of customers, however, made life more difficult for the pubs and shopkeepers and this was followed by some changes that were a bit over-zealous. The Urban Council were conscious that they had been doing a good job rehousing slum dwellers, and that there was a long queue for the new council houses. As a newly married couple we were in the queue but managed to buy a house in Roseway in 1953 before being offered a council one. At the time Compulsory Purchase Orders were easy to obtain and some well built houses and viable businesses were demolished unnecessarily.

A recent look showed that most buildings were sheltered housing and looked well taken care of. Only three pubs remained, one of which was closed. The busiest business seemed to be James Rollason's. Jim was in my class at Princes Street School and I'm pleased his business prospers. Likewise the Sign Shop, Farr and Harris (recently expanded) and several other shops including a pet's grooming business that has been a brush maker and a Chinese laundry, appear quite prosperous. Austin's, where I was born, no longer sells newspapers. Just a few of the best of the old houses near the New Church Road junction have survived and look well cared for. The old Wesleyan Chapel became its Sunday School, the Chad Valley toy factory, then an antiques shop and is now well converted to flats. The most attractive new building is undoubtedly Harry Edwards and Sons, Funeral Directors on the corner with Victoria Road.

My little wander along the street on a cold, windy day, showed that almost, but not quite everything had changed, not only from the 1920s but also from the 1950s. Well, that's the nature of things; change is normal, staying the same would be boring. The street is full of surprises with buildings bustling with trade; businesses expanding and some packing up. One group of buildings is gently rotting and waiting for the bulldozers while others show signs of prosperity.

My 1934 Wellington Directory lists each building and names its occupant and his business if any. There was a mixture of houses and shops as there is now, numbering from New Street to the junction with Mill Bank and King Street, with 147 addresses, odd numbers on the left, even on the right. Our old shop was 49 (I remember because I was taught it in case I was lost) and it's now 45.

The commercial firms on the left included Avery, scale manufacturers, Hesketh, boot maker, Duke's Head, Percy Price, Hairdresser, Mrs. P Price, Lodging house, Elizabeth Clayton, Hairdresser, Thomas Smith, Brush Maker, Tom Austin, Newsagent (that's the birthplace), Miss Smith, Draper, Harry Edwards, Joiner and Undertaker, Frank Tinsley, Grocer, John H Briscoe, Hardware Dealer, Berry & Warmington, Scale Makers, Oddfellows Arms, Mrs. Bytheway, B Robertson, Hairdresser, James Beard, Tripe Dresser, Arthur Griffiths, Window Cleaner, W Johnson & Sons, Hardware Dealer, Miss L Phillips, Confectioner, John Twinney, Boot Maker, WH Duce, Fried Fish Saloon, W Davies, Hairdresser, Mrs A Waltho, confectioner, Kings Head Inn, George Jones, Walter Magness, Plumber and Charles Magness, Confectioner (the Boys' High School 'tuck shop').

On the right were: Agnes Harvey, Grocer, Frederick Rushton, Chimney Sweep, Richard Weston, Boot maker, John H Jones, Boot maker, Mrs M Downes, Nelson Inn, Charles Hitchen, Boot maker, Mrs Betsy Clarke, Lodging House, Thomas Palin, Fishmonger, Herbert Owen, Draper, F Leake & Co, Furniture Manufacturers, JTH Purcell, Grocer, W Williams, Hand and Hart Inn, JC Holding, General Dealer, Tom Roberts, Landscape Gardener and Mrs. Barker, Tobacconist.

All the rest of the buildings were private houses, most of them rented from a great variety of owners. There will be a few older readers who may remember some of the names quoted, possibly even some who are related to them. I must ask my friend Allan Frost when his grandfather, Noah, came and set up his bakers' business in High Street; in the 1950s we thought it had been there forever, selling their delicious crusty bread. This was so good he's even had a new row of houses named after him.

Naturally High Street has changed and for most of the inhabitants it has been for the better. Those who live in the (relatively) new flats and maisonettes are in far better conditions than people were in the tatty cramped slums and should be glad, though a few perfectly good buildings were demolished too. Hurrah for High Street.

GROCERS' SHOPS LONG AGO

What I remember most about the old fashioned grocers' shops we had before supermarkets overtook us is the smell. Actually there were many different smells. Remember this was before the advent of fridges and freezers and lots of eatables had much more pronounced smells that have been frozen over nowadays. As Rudyard Kipling said of a cake in one of his 'Just So' stories, "It smelled most sentimental".

There was a wonderful collection of scents and aromas coming at you when you entered a grocers' shop. Different cheeses, different teas, butter, lard, bacon, sausages, pepper, salt, mustard, cakes jam, jelly and so on, all mixing with the pipe and cigarette smoke of the men customers; women (or at least ladies) didn't smoke in public. Across The Square was a 'posh' shop, Richard Britain, which catered for wealthier customers than us. That smelled strongly and deliciously of freshly roasted coffee that we couldn't afford.

Occasionally my mother sent me to JC Lloyd's grocery shop in Wellington Market Square with a brown wickerwork basket and a list of things she needed for the week. She also gave me a ten shilling note to pay for them. I hung the basket on the handlebars of my Raleigh bike (a proper 'sit up and beg' job with stirrup brakes that paused to think for a while after you jammed them on before it stopped). Hanging a shopping basket on your bike isn't recommended but other than ride one-handed, where else does the thing go?

At the time I'm thinking of I was about 13 to 16. No, I wasn't a teenager; the word hadn't been invented (or more likely imported from America) like all my age-group I've never been a teenager. Not that we were any different of course, we had all the symptoms of today's teenagers. I was clumsy, awkward, self centred, shy and noisy. I behaved as if I knew it all whilst realising that actually I knew very little.

So I leaned my bike against Lloyds' shop window and stalked in, trying to look confident, which I really wasn't. The shop was square with customers in the middle and counters manned by staff, mostly girls, around on three sides, the fourth being the entrance and shop display windows. The girls all looked smart and wore white aprons. They were various ages; I tried to pick a young one of my own age. They ranged from school leavers of 14 upwards to very old ones who must have been almost 50. In those days before the Last World War people didn't live as long as they do now and anyway a youngster's perspective is different. Women have to be at least 90 before I think of them as being old nowadays.

Having picked my assistant girl I gave her the list and the basket. It was her job (not mine as it is with supermarkets) to go and find the things on the list and put them in the basket. As she bustled round the ship, bringing sugar, flour and so on, I tried to chat her up of course. That's not a skill I excelled in and I often found myself confused and red faced. I had no sister, my Elementary School in Wrockwardine had been all boys and Wellington Boys High School, where I now attended, was separated from the girls' school by a 15 foot wall. There was clearly a lot to be learned about girls.

Sugar, flour and such were kept in big hundredweight sacks and had to be weighed out into blue paper bags for each customer on scales with two pans, one for the goods and one for the brass weights. In every case instructions were clear, that I must see that the weight was correct and if there was a choice of brands, then the cheapest was best. Every penny mattered; it was, after all, 1 /120th of my ten shillings, and the more change I took home the better. Bacon was cut from a flitch hanging from the ceiling sliced on the machine and we always had to have cut 6; a thin slice which 'went farther'. You could say we were 'penny pinching'. We couldn't afford not to be.

Before the War there were very many grocers' shops in Wellington. There are 42 advertised in the Wellington Directory of 1934. How many supermarkets have we to choose from now? Is it four or five? Of course they're much, much bigger and relative to modern incomes the cost of groceries is probably quite a bit less. Very few people went shopping in a car in the old days, simply because they didn't have one and modern hatchbacks, like plastic bags, refrigeration, decimal coinage, plastic money, computer tills, shopping trolleys and shop car parks hadn't been invented. Also the grocery business had not been taken over by the huge international multi-billion pound firms who own most of the world's supermarkets hadn't evolved.

There have been vast in the grocery trade during my lifetime; some are improvements, others are boring. There was very little difference between the prices shops charged for the same quality goods just like nowadays. The two biggest changes have been in the size and the ownership of the shops. Pre-war shops were relatively tiny, often only the size of a sitting room and there was usually one owner who ran his (seldom her) shop personally.

If readers want to look up the grocers' shops in Wellington back when there were over 40 of them, the information will be found in various directories, many of which are in the local studies section at Wellington library. Readers in the other local towns and villages should ask at their local library; if they're not there then just ask why not and where to find them. They're fascinating repositories of local history and should be more used.

The old grocer is an extinct species. You decide if this is good or bad.

GARDENS, THEN AND NOW

Every morning I go to collect my daily paper, passing neighbours' gardens/ car parks. They are enormously varied and some are very beautiful. My family have had an even greater variety of gardens to enjoy and work in. This morning it occurred to me that readers might like a short ramble about gardens, so here goes.

People talk about old fashioned cottage gardens and often miss the whole point of them. The country cottage garden existed, not as a casual hobby or a pretty background for the house or even as a space to sunbathe and play with the kids; it was the main provider of food for the family. There may have been roses round the door but vegetables, chickens, pigs and fruit trees were its most important contents. Without a decent sized garden the old farm workers would have starved because of their low wages. The nearest I've seen for many years to a real cottage garden is at Blists Hill Museum round the Squatter's Cottage.

Pleasure gardens were only for the rich. They could have huge parks laid out by men like Capability Brown and walled kitchen gardens employing dozens of gardeners. Have a walk round Attingham or Dudmaston to see what I mean. More recently up-and-coming business men could make smaller versions like Sunnycroft in Wellington, which is also worth a visit. Perhaps the nearest to the Sunnycroft garden are in 'YUPPY' (young upwardly mobile) houses, mainly in local villages. Now most people in my part of Wellington have beautiful gardens of one kind or another.

My father had a very productive vegetable garden at Orleton Cottage, by the cricket pitch. He would have been ashamed to buy vegetables except exotics like bananas, though his friend Percy Thrower grew them in Shrewsbury. There are still a few folks who grow their own vegetables and swank about their freshness. It's hard work though and I have given up years ago, even though I envy their crisp veggies. In fact I can see a few 'proper' gardens from our house. Certainly they have a point; growing your own has many advantages, despite being hard work and perhaps more expensive than 'shop bought'. I gather that there's an upsurge in allotment gardening and Wellington needs, and may soon have, a new allotment garden.

My son Paul has worked at gardening as well as radio and newspaper writing. After a spell with the National Trust he went off to America to help design a really big garden- one thousand three hundred acres of it! Once he was asked what kind of garden he would like to have and replied, "Kazakhstan". His present garden is long, large, beautiful and hidden; a wonderful playground for his grandchildren.

My son Mark and his wife Jayne took over a garden from a market gardener. It had several huge plastic greenhouses and was waiting for someone to come along and turn it into something more interesting, which they did. Their present garden has a gate onto the Longmynd, which they frequently use as an extension as they are both keen walkers.

Many neighbours enjoy the Bowring Rec., and especially The Wrekin Forest as part of their space; that is especially true of the dog walkers among them. Some encourage wildlife; others will do almost anything to eliminate any living thing they have not bought, planted or invited. My own garden is meant to encourage wild things, though I confess to not being friendly to some of the visiting cats because they prey on or frighten the birds encouraged by our bird tables. There are wild bees, ants, beetles, frogs, newts, butterflies and no end of other wild creatures. They don't bother us and we let them be.

One of the things I like is weeds. It's interesting to see what comes up if you let it and only zap it if you have too many of the same sort or if it gets too big. Like most English gardens the land was once forest and if you leave it alone that's what you get. We have lived here for over 30 years and in that time yew, oak, ash, beech, rowan, cherry, plum, elm, lilac, holly, birch, elder, hawthorn and hazel have all appeared and made their home here. Some may one day become a problem – but not in my lifetime.

Some older readers might remember Miss Carver's house, now replaced by Carver's Close, which was left neglected for many years, with ivy and trees growing out of the building and all over the garden until the house was falling down. That's exactly what will happen to any piece of ground where Nature is allowed to have its own way. The Ercall quarries opposite Buckatree Hotel were once a moonscape but the landscape has been recolonised by the forest and this is a fascinating study for anyone interested in biology. It's a wonderful example of the power of nature.

Of course even nature-nuts like me have to draw a line. I mow a central lawn at the back for important functions, like kids playing, sunbathing, tea parties and reading. I wanted the garden to be like a glade in a forest and it's coming on nicely but Naomi, my wife, likes flowers so we have to compromise a bit. Besides, we have to protect the house from the effects of the trees.

"The Ercall quarries opposite Buckatree Hotel were once a moonscape but the landscape has been recolonised by the forest and this is a fascinating study for anyone interested in biology. It's a wonderful example of the power of nature"

CHANGING OUR WORLD

Does anyone still remember the words to a little song in the film, 'South Pacific'? They went, "You got to have a dream. If you don't have a dream, how you gonna have a dream come true?" I think we all have dreams; things we hope for and dream about for a long time. Some of them are quite ordinary, just involving ourselves and our family and others are very big indeed and would change the whole world if they happened. Some of them are fantasies, never likely to come true but others we pursue and work at until, maybe after a very long and exhausting time, our dream becomes reality.

"Think globally, act locally" is a very good motto. I've been wanting to 'do something' for World Peace and ending the crass stupidity of wars for a very long time; since I wrote a long letter to the League of Nations in 1939 just before the Last World War started and I was 16 at the time. Of course they took no notice, though there was nothing they could have done anyway.

As I write one of my dreams is beginning to come to fruition – Wellington Peace Garden. By the time this article is printed and delivered we shall have our garden, belonging to all us ordinary people of Wellington, though this is being written the Sunday before it opens. Will there be a good crowd there?

I have several dreams about how it will be used. Some of these involve many people who may well have other ideas. Would some or all of the local churches like to use it to promote World Peace? I hope so. Will our local Muslims plant a Damask rose to remind everyone that theirs is a peaceful religion? They have been invited to do so. What will local schools and colleges do? String peace messages from the trees? I have heard of Lions, Rotarians and other friendly organisations who said they would like to contribute. There is talk of some local Germans commemorating those who were killed in the last World War. Perhaps some of the local Japanese and Italians may like to do the same.

In 1917 my father was shot as he was fighting in France. He wasn't killed (or there would have been no me) but he suffered from his wounds for the rest of his life. He only survived because he was dealt with by a particularly skilful surgeon. Doesn't he deserve to be honoured? Also in 1917 my mother was returning from Jamaica in a 'banana boat' that was sunk in mid-Atlantic by a submarine. She also was very nearly a war casualty. Does this merit commemoration?

There must be many other Wellingtonians whose ancestors, not on the War Memorial because they were not killed in action, but who served like the rest of us, should be remembered and who think contributing to the Peace Garden is the right way to do that. We also forget the civilians who lost their lives in war; here's a chance to commemorate.

Many quite innocent people have been killed in wartime of many nationalities, often that had nothing to do with the war. I watched as Caen was shelled and bombed in 1944 by huge numbers of our guns and bombers. There were no German casualties but many French civilians were killed and wounded by our shells and bombs.

Incidentally, there are many new phrases that annoy me but the worst is, "Friendly fire". Believe me, and I do know what I'm talking about, there is absolutely nothing 'friendly' about being attacked by your own side. What idiot thought up the expression, "Friendly Fire"? My guess is that he (surely not a woman) was a desk-bound civilian employee of the Pentagon. Please don't use the words in my hearing or I might forget I'm a pacifist. I have been bombed by the American

Air Force and the RAF, fired on by the Royal Navy and the Royal Artillery and seen friends killed and wounded by 'our side'. Call it accident if you like or 'cock-up' or incompetence or stupidity but never friendly.

Sorry about that interjection. The thought just drifted into my little bald head and I had to let it out. Better now.

Another part of the same dream is that Wellington can become an example of how to set up a Peace Garden that will be copied in many other places. There must be lots of councils who would like to do something good for their towns without spending public money. It's such a simple little idea and it seems to work well. Local councils all own bits of land in town centres like this that can only be a bit of garden or a scruffy tip. Handing these patches of land to locals with a dream can work anywhere.

There are several other Peace Gardens in other towns; you can find them on the web. My grandson says there's a good one in Manchester and I've seen the one in Coventry. The garden in Hiroshima looks particularly wonderful. We even have a garden in Telford, given by Japanese people. All of these are different from ours because they cost a lot of money and ours costs nothing but the price of the plants we will put in and the work of willing volunteers who will look after it. Besides, it will belong to all the 20,000 people of Wellington. Gosh! I hope they don't all turn up at once!

My late father-in-law, Bill Hurdley, had a lovely expression for things that would last longer than him, "It'll see me out." Wellington Peace Garden will see me out.

"I think we all have dreams; things we hope for and dream about for a long time. Some of them are quite ordinary, just involving ourselves and our family and others are very big indeed and would change the whole world if they happened"

06 PEACE AND HEALTH

REMEMBERING WAR AND PEACE

The other day I attended a meeting to organise this year's Remembrance Parade in Wellington. There will be a few changes, mainly because the parade and public will be on the grass of the churchyard facing southwest to the ceremonies at the Lych Gate instead of being squashed on Church Street. We all thought this was a good move and will make life better for the smaller children, who will find it easier to see what is going on, and we old folks will have less trouble with the steps.

In the 1920s there was a great upsurge of War Memorial building. The objects were to honour and remember the many that had been killed defending their country, to respect those who had suffered and returned, like my father and mother, and to remind everyone of the horrors of war. This was after the 'Great War to end all wars', as it was referred to. In honouring and respecting those who had taken part in the war the memorial, parades and services were a success but unfortunately people soon forgot about how horrible the war had been and how stupid was the loss of so many lives.

Time went by and another world war loomed. I remember well the national feeling of horror but that it seemed inevitable. My parents' generation prepared to help on the 'home front' with the Home Guard, munitions factories, food production, fire watching and so on. My own generation expected to be 'called up' for military service and sent off to fight against similar people to ourselves, who had been conscripted by our country's enemies. Even those of us who recognised the sheer monumental stupidity of going off to murder our government's enemies' thought of the whole thing as inevitable. We felt there was no way out, so we went off and did our duty.

Long after coming home from the last World War as I prefer to call it, I wrote the following little verse to sum up my thoughts on Remembrance Day:

I REMEMBER MY FRIENDS
AND MY ENEMIES TOO.
WE ALL DID OUR DUTY TO OUR COUNTRIES
AND SLAUGHTERED EACH OTHER.
ISN'T WAR STUPID?

For many years after the last World War there were parades in Wellington with bands and marching men and women, boys and girls. Those who had lost their lives were honoured at the service by the Lych Gate memorial on Remembrance Day and a good sized parade marched and saluted the Chairman of the Council.

Then, in 1974, Wellington lost its Urban Council in a reorganisation and there was no leadership to organise the parade. It was not until 1988, when we were granted a parish council (which promptly declared itself a Town Council) and we had some sort of leadership for the town, that parades were started again. Since then the popularity of Remembrance has steadily grown and we again pay proper homage to the men of our town killed in the two World Wars and all the other wars our country has been fighting in since then.

Here I would like to thank the organisers, Town Council, the Parade Marshall, Wellington Town Band and all the hundreds who have joined in and supported the event.

For many years we have also, in Wellington, held a little ceremony at 11am on 11th of November to commemorate Armistice Day whenever it is not on Remembrance Sunday. This is in Market Square, consisting of some recorded music, Last Post, two minutes silence, Reveille, the Act of Remembrance ('They shall grow not old...), the Kohima Epitaph and the National Anthem. The Mayor will be there, with the standard bearers of the Royal British Legion and, I hope, a good crowd of Wellingtonians.

Wellington has succeeded with its ceremonies, which for many years have been very well attended. Scouts and Guides come in large numbers, as do many other organisations, including the Cadet forces. As an old soldier I have to admit that the Air Force Cadets are very smart, as indeed are many others. We seem not to have attracted many serving soldiers, sailors or airmen lately and veterans of the Last World War are getting thin on the ground. Our parade, despite being largely ignored and unreported in the local media, is a large and fine one, well worth coming to watch.

Some people, however, are unjustly forgotten or ignored. A large number of civilians have been killed and wounded in war. They should be remembered too. So should our ex-enemies.

Now here's a little idea to stimulate thought. Remember Harry Patch, the last surviving Great War fighter? He said, "War is stupid," and he was right. All the people I have met who have actually been in battles agree with him. We remember just how horrible war really is; there's nothing heroic in killing people.

This year Wellington's parade will move off from Naylor's Row car park at 10.25am, march down New Street, through Market Square to All Saints Church. We expect a parade of 500 with 200 spectators on the grass in the churchyard. After the service we will march back, saluting the Mayor in Market Square.

The Memorials and the Parades do a good job of reminding us of 'the fallen'. It is important that we should honour them. But they don't fulfil the other function that their originators hoped they would; they don't prevent war. We have been at war almost every year since the last World War. This is wrong. We should be living in peace with our neighbours.

"We remember just how horrible war really is;
there's nothing heroic in killing people"

WELLINGTON PEACE GARDEN
THOUGHTS FROM THE PEACE GARDENERS

Our purpose is to create a beautiful garden in Wellington town centre, where we can plant to show our commitment to peace and the end of armed conflict.

We are grateful to T&W Council for allocating the land and Wellington Town Council for their support. Please help us to plant the garden.

It's a long strip of land opposite the entrance to the new library next to the swimming pool. We hope it will soon be full of beautiful plants.

WHO IS IT FOR?

We hope to see many local organisations including churches and other religious bodies and those with no specific religious views, schools and colleges, together with all the many clubs, associations and groups in the town planning their own events and planting for peace.

We also welcome individuals and families to plant in remembrance of their loved ones or simply to make the place more beautiful.

REGULATIONS

1. There are no regulations. We prefer to trust common sense.
2. Please just have a good long think about what you plant.
3. If you're sure it's right, it probably is.
4. Don't forget to plant carefully and add water.
5. We'd rather you looked after your plant yourself
6. We'll give you a label to pop in the ground; write it yourself.

IT'S FOR ALL OF US

Should anyone dominate the garden? We think not, and that does include us. It's a bit ridiculous to start a fight about who's the most peaceful don't you think? Our garden should just grow as it is planted; it isn't being planned.

LET'S PLANT A BEAUTIFUL GARDEN AND BE PROUD

HELP WHEN IT'S NEEDED

This year we have been needing quite a lot of assistance from various organisations. Naomi, my wife, became very ill in June and died in November. This involved our GP, Shropdoc, the ambulance service, the Princess Royal Hospital (several different wards and specialists), our new GP, Social Services, the Community Nurses, Macmillan Nurse and the Hospice at Home service (with Marie Curie) of Severn Hospice. That's a great number of different bodies involved but they all played their part, mostly very well indeed.

Also, of course, we needed a lot of support from our very diverse family and friends, who rallied round wonderfully well in their unique ways. We're most grateful to them for the tremendous way they upheld us and of course we helped each other a lot. Religion is important too – if you have one. Naomi belonged to the Church of England and I am a Quaker; Joyce and Sonja have been valuable supporters. However, this article is about the helping professions and what they did for us when we needed them.

The first point of call in illness is your doctor; here we found problems. It was difficult making appointments, especially for home visits, with Wellington Practice, with whom we had been since they opened. Perhaps they're too popular and overburdened. When I wanted a non-urgent appointment the waiting time was five weeks; I thought that was far longer than it should have been. The doctors were fine but their system failed us. Eventually we transferred to Malling Health Wrekin, near PRH hospital, where Drs Walton and Grey have been excellent and most caring. We couldn't have asked for a better service. While writing this, Dr Walton rang, just to ask how I was coping; she is becoming a kind friend as well as my GP.

When eventually Naomi went to the Princess Royal Hospital, diagnosed to be suffering from pneumonia, it was a weekend but the help she received initially at the MAU unit was good. Sometimes there seemed to be communication problems between different sections/units/professions but perhaps that's to be expected. So is the food situation; however good it is, it doesn't help if the patient can't eat it and patients eat little because they are ill. She was transferred to Ward 8, then to Ward 14 as the result of further diagnoses and it became clear that there was more than one problem. The nursing care varied between good and excellent. Visiting times were fine, though the journeys twice a day for a month made the hospital not two miles away but 240 miles in total.

A silly mistake occurred when she was rushed off to Shrewsbury for an endoscopic examination, only to discover that the RSH had not made an appointment for her. It was ironic that the endoscope at the PRH eventually revealed that she had a cancer. She was chairman of the League of Friends when they paid for the first endoscope some years ago. She was determined to be out of hospital in time for a party to celebrate our Diamond Wedding and convinced everyone they should let her go.

After the party she needed full time care but, willing as I was, I couldn't cope alone. Naomi knew what the outcome was likely to be and opted to stay at home. The caring professions then mobilised (perhaps rounded up by Dr Walton) and moved into action. Social Services, so often criticised recently for doing too much or too little, provided a lot of help after we had done a little 'tick-boxing', answering questions from their remote controllers. Like a lot of organisations we found no problem with the people who did the work but some irritation with those who wrote the regulations. It seemed so silly that two intelligent men who brought a hospital bed were forbidden to move our furniture out of the way. The carers of the Rapid Response team and of Debbie's DH Homecare who later took over were most praiseworthy. Lots of equipment was delivered and later collected very efficiently.

Community Nurses Kate, Maureen and Carole came regularly. They were not just efficient professionals but very human, friendly and helpful 'above the call of duty' as it sometimes says on medal citations. But despite all this I was finding life very difficult as the only person there '24/7'. It was becoming too much. At this point the Hospice at Home service, run by Dawn, Maggie and Mel, offered help at night from 10pm to 7am, enabling me to sleep and saving my remaining bit of sanity.

These lovely people, Stephanie, Amanda, Georgina and Vera came and sat through the night looking after Naomi, checking, listening and caring so that I could get some rest. They woke me with a cup of tea at 7am, reporting on how the night had gone. I'd asked them to wake me if anything changed and Vera came at 5am on the last day to say Naomi's breathing had altered. She was quite right and the end came 12 hours later. They were so kind. Hospice at Home depends on charity, unlike most of the others. Our family and friends have given generously and I hope enabled others to have the help they gave us.

So Naomi was able to be at home, as she wanted, in her last days, instead of either hospital or hospice. It still wasn't easy for her or us, her family, but all these good people made it possible. Far too often we hear grumbles about the NHS and Social Services, about hospitals and health centres, about doctors, surgeons, nurses and carers and how social workers never seem to 'get it right'; our experience shows the opposite.

Of course our family and many friends have kept us going and are still keeping me going but readers may like to know what help is available. I hope this account will help others who find themselves in a similar situation; we must all accept the inevitable eventually.

"I hope this account will help others who find themselves in a similar situation; we must all accept the inevitable eventually"

07 HISTORY

RELIGIONS ROUND THE WREKIN

To my mind, one of the most interesting things about the human race is that we are all different. Long ago, when I was a lad, there were just a few religious differences in Wellington; you were Church of England, Methodist, Baptist or Roman Catholic and that was it. Nowadays there are far more choices. Even my own religion has changed over the years. I was christened in New Street Methodist Church, then confirmed in the Church of England at St Peters, Wrockwardine and for a time regularly attended Christ Church, Wellington. Nearly twenty years ago I became a Quaker (a member of the Religious Society of Friends), which I still am. I'm convinced that we should respect each other's right to be different so you won't find any criticism of other faiths here.

Please forgive me for concentrating on Wellington; it's the place I know best and if I included all the religious buildings in the whole county of The Wrekin this would be a boring list. Still most people round The Wrekin are, or consider themselves, Christian, though a large number seldom attend their church except for weddings and funerals. Perhaps the most common religious belief is agnostic and there are many atheists.

The largest Christian church is All Saints Church, which is Church of England, Evangelical in its outlook. It has the oldest building, built in 1790, to replace an older church going back to at least the 13th Century.

Christ Church in New Church Road is Anglo-Catholic. It was built as a Chapel of Ease in 1839 and changed from Evangelical to Anglo-Catholic by its Vicar, Rev. JP Abbey. There are several other old and new Anglican churches in surrounding towns and villages.

The Methodist Church in New Street, a new building on the old site, also serves many social functions; again the district has many more. A few years ago an older building was demolished because of the high cost of maintenance. The building was less important than the congregation.

St Patrick's Roman Catholic Church has recently had an increase in numbers and some masses are now said in Polish. A previous Catholic church in Mill Bank became a school, then a cinema and has been demolished.

The Union Free Church in Constitution Hill has a joint membership of Baptists and Congregationists. It has an interesting similarity to St Patrick's – both were planned with a spire and neither spires were added because of the cost.

One recent Christian church is the House of Prayer held in the old Town Hall over the market. There may be other 'house churches' in the area – I don't know.

A lively Pentecostal Church on Tan Bank has mainly (but not exclusively) Afro-Caribbean members. Their building was originally the Sunday school of the Primitive Methodists, who merged with Wesleyan Methodists in New Street. It's called the First Church of Jesus Christ Apostolic.

The Church of Jesus Christ of Latter-day Saints or Mormons in Glebe Street has increased numbers and has added a new building in Lawley. Jehovah's Witnesses meet at Plough Road, Wrockwardine Wood and Springfield Christian Fellowship at Tweedale Industrial Estate.

The Salvation Army meets in Lion Street, Oakengates and has buildings of various kinds throughout the area serving their work with those in need, as well as a shop in Wellington.

Some Greek Orthodox worshipers have joined the Anglican churches but the Serbian Orthodox

Church has a church in Donnington. Many are the descendants of European Voluntary Workers who came here after the Last World War.

There is an old tradition of charismatic preachers round The Wrekin, including John Fletcher, Vicar of Madeley, Dr Cranage in Wellington and the Ketley man, S Parkes Cadman, who began the tradition of popular radio preachers in America.

In Telford's 'Town Centre' is Meeting Point House, where we Quakers meet. There are, I'm told, five other churches in the same building including an Anglican/Methodist church, some Nigerian Christians and a Chinese Christian church whom I have heard singing traditional English Christmas Carols delightfully in Chinese.

Probably the fastest growing religious group is Islam. There are three Mosques in Wellington; the main one in Tan Bank used to be a Primitive Methodist Church. Also there is another that is growing from a house in Regent Street and a third Islamic Centre in the old Drill Hall, in King Street. The first I visited was at Christ Church Hall, where newly arrived Muslims met for Eid ul Fitr and I was able to welcome them.

There are also large numbers of Sikhs in our area, who have their Guru Nanak Sikh Gurdwara in the old school building in Hadley. The Sikh community gave generously to the Friends of the Princess Royal Hospital, presenting the chairman, my late wife, with a cheque.

I do not know where Hindus meet; please tell me if you do. There are a few Buddhists also in Hadley including an old friend DD Ahir. Jews have no local Synagogue and the few local ones I know visit a Synagogue in Wolverhampton. There is a Spiritualist church in Watling Street I'm told.

Over the years I have attended services at Methodist, Anglican, Roman Catholic, Congregational, Baptist, Mormon and Pentecostal churches as well as my own Quaker meetings. Also I've visited Muslim Mosques and Sikh Gurdwaras. I have always found the people friendly, welcoming and peaceful.

All the religions I know and most people with no religion support the idea of peace.

We can show our commitment to peace, by having no enemies or we can, quietly, with no fuss or getting permission, honour the life of someone we were fond of. We can plant something in Wellington Peace Garden.

The garden is in front of the new library and it's beginning to be beautiful in spring. It will cost you the plant and the effort of planting it; that's all. Just do what you think is right; it probably is.

Peace, Pax, Pace, Salam, Shalom, Frieden.

"We can show our commitment to peace, by having no enemies or we can, quietly, with no fuss or getting permission, honour the life of someone we were fond of"

WELLINGTON RAILWAY STATION

Some time during the late 1870s my maternal grandfather came down from Chester to work on the signals at Wellington station, which was relatively new, having been opened in 1849. In those days working for the railway companies was reckoned to be a good steady job. He worked at No. 1 box on the 'up line' near the bridge in Mill Lane, off Regent Street until he retired, about 1923. He was very proud of 'his' company, the Great Western (GWR 'God's Wonderful Railway') and scathing of the other company operating in Wellington, London Midland and Scottish (LMS or 'ell of a mess').

Gramp, as I called him, used to take me when he visited the station to see some of his old colleagues and inspect the place. There was a wooden cabin at the end of the bay, where the porters waited for customers. The place was full of a thick fug of pipe smoke with a big round coke stove in the middle where a kettle was always boiling for making tea, which was incredibly strong with lots of sugar.

Trains were on time. Gramp was amazed one day when a 'through train', the Zulu, was six minutes late. That event was discussed for several years afterwards. He always wore his railway watch on its gold chain across his waistcoat to check the times, which were nearly always precisely correct. He took me to his box, with its array of big levers that operated the signals and points that required much effort to pull. We listened to the tinkling sound of the telegraph and he translated its messages and watched as the signalman pressed the little red key, replying to the message coming down the line, relaying them to the box at the station. Unsurprisingly the signal-box was full of pipe smoke.

There were five platforms, mostly busy, as Wellington was the main junction for East Shropshire. Lines went to Shrewsbury and Wolverhampton as now, but also to Market Drayton/Crewe, Hadley and Newport, Hadley/Coalport and Ketley/Coalbrookdale/Much Wenlock/Craven Arms. There were many small stations; Shrewsbury trains went through Admaston, Walcott and Upton Magna. The two platforms in the bay were for local trains. One train from Wolverhampton had a slip coach on the back which was uncoupled at speed a few miles away and continued behind the train on its own momentum, being guided into the bay by a signalman's points change. It had a driver with no engine but a brake.

The old steam trains made a very satisfying array of noises, whistling, steaming, screaming, swooshing, thundering, rumbling and the soporific 'tiddle-di-dum' of the wheels over the rail-joints. Big ones shook the ground, especially the 'through-expresses' that travelled on the middle rails and treated Wellington with disdain. Goods trains were often very long and slow, pottering through the station with their assorted trucks, vans and carriages.

During the War the many trains to and from Donnington 'dump' carried military secrets under tarpaulin sheets. On Mondays cattle wagons took beef 'on the hoof' from the Smithfield, protesting loudly that they just wanted to go home and weren't happy. Grooms timber yard, the cattle market, Gough's coal-wharf and so on had their own sidings the other side of Church Street bridge in Wellington Goods Station. Here various trucks and vans were juggled and shunted about by fussy little shunting engines until they were made into trains going in the right direction. We stood on the tin bridge watching the fascinating process of truck shuffling. All the big factories and mines, like Sankeys and Granville, had their own sidings and often their own trucks. Small parcels came in to the parcels office at the passenger station but the big stuff went to the goods station.

On the north side of the station were a lot of big work sheds. It was fascinating to watch a big heavy engine carefully driven on the turntable, still steaming, and some men would pull it round to face the opposite way. Another shed was full of coal and coke and there were men working all the while, cleaning, polishing and looking after the great steam engines. Most of the carriages were kept neat and clean by a squad of women, who swept, dusted, polished and scrubbed them. If the carriages weren't clean it wasn't their fault.

Water was important to the engines and there was a tall water tower, a large metal tank supported by a high blue brick base, to ensure a reliable supply. Between the rails were troughs filled with water, so that 'through' trains could suck up water as they thundered past. In bad weather small devises shaped like wrist watches were fastened on the rails which made a small explosion to warn of the approach of a train in thick fog.

Many people worked at the station, all with their special blue uniforms that clearly showed their occupation and rank; overalls for the cleaners and a very smart suit for the Stationmaster who was an extremely grand person. Some wore buttonholes, especially in the summer. One ticket collector had a tiny vase that fitted into his buttonhole that always contained a rose bud. There was a great deal of pride in working on the railways; jobs were steady and each carried responsibilities for a particular part of the system.

Since those days three mistakes have been made which upset an excellent service. First it was Nationalisation, which reduced competition; second was Beeching, the cutting and demolition of many stations and tracks and third was Privatisation, which resulted in lost jobs and wealth for greedy incompetents. Improvements in cars, lorries, buses and roads also led to the decline of the railways.

Now Wellington railway station is picking itself up. Passenger numbers are twice what they were last year. The few staff left are cheerful, efficient and helpful, like the excellent Platelayer cafe. As petrol prices rise there's hope that some at least of the prestige of the railways may return.

"The old steam trains made a very satisfying array of noises, whistling, steaming, screaming, swooshing, thundering, rumbling and the soporific 'tiddle-di-dum' of the wheels over the rail-joints"

WHAT'S THAT IN OLD MONEY?

Let's get this straight first – comparing prices and wages in old and new money is like trying to measure your waist with a piece of elastic. For example, in the 1930s there was a firm called FST – the Fifty Shilling Tailor. They would sell you a smart, 'off the peg' suit for fifty shillings; that's two pounds ten shillings. Oh, £2.50? Yes if you like, but that was a skilled craftsman's weekly wages. Now you can easily find a cheap suit like mine for £100. Try to employ a craftsman on £100 a week! So you see, a modern suit is cheaper.

The other day the Chancellor of the Exchequer announced that he was taking 'one pence' off the tax on a pint of beer. How ignorant can you get? The word 'pence' is plural; he meant one penny. Someone in the Treasury should have told him. In old money, 1p = 2.4d because there were 240 pence in the pound. Some older readers will remember when money changed; we suspected traders (not without good cause) of using it as an excuse to raise prices.

For the benefit of youngsters who have always used decimal coinage (some of whom must be nearly pensionable) let me explain how things were. There were four farthings or two halfpence in a penny, twelve pennies (48 farthings or 24 halfpennies) in a shilling and twenty shillings (960 farthings, 480 halfpence or 240 pence) in a pound.

Coins included (copper) a farthing, a halfpenny, a penny, (silver) a three penny bit, a sixpence (tanner), a shilling (bob), a florin (two shilling piece) a half crown (two shillings and six pence) and (gold) a half sovereign (ten shillings) and sovereign (pound). Later there were notes for ten shillings and one pound. At one time the three penny bit changed from silver to copper/bronze. As the song went, "Rule Britannia, two tanners make a bob; three make eighteen pence and four two bob".

Then a marriage licence cost seven shillings and sixpence. What's the least number of coins to pay for one? In how many different ways could you be given the change from half a sovereign? And when the church asked for a 'silver collection' what's the least you can put on the plate? Rich kids (not me) had sixpence a week pocket money. How many gobstoppers at a farthing each was that?

By now, if you didn't know before, you will have guessed that I was a teacher. In those far off, good old days I had an answer book, which was far more use than a cane.

Everybody learned their tables; not just the 2 x 1 = 2 sort but also the 'How many ounces in a pound, pounds in a stone, stones in a hundredweight, hundredweights in a ton? How many yards in a chain, chains in a furlong and furlongs in a mile, miles in a league? And don't forget acres, pints, quarts, gallons, pecks, bushels and all sorts of much more quirky ways of measuring things. However did we manage? Wasn't it daft?

No, actually, the old ways of measuring were not as daft as you may think. For instance, an inch is about the width of a man's thumb, a span (9 inches) is from thumb to little finger, a league is an hour's walk, a pint is enough to drink with dinner. Most of the old measures were in human terms. I still try to keep my weight between 12 stones 7 pounds and 13 stones because that was what I weighed 70 years ago in the Army. Mind you it's not muscle any more and it's in different places. On the old 'inch to a mile' walking maps it was easy to count the thumb widths along a road and know how many miles it was.

At my secondary school we used both systems naturally. Metrics were for the science subjects like physics and chemistry and the traditional English system for everything else. Of course we had to use metrics for French; that's why some people call the decimal system 'Napoleon's Revenge', thinking that although he lost the war to us (with German help) he got his own back by imposing his metrics on us.

Here's something few people know. Not even the older chaps. Thomas Parker, a forgotten genius from Coalbrookdale, who invented an enormous list of wonderful things, tried to popularise his own decimal system based on a cubic inch. He always carried one in his pocket. Anyone interested should start in Coalbrookdale Church and inspect his plaque. I'll say no more; do your own research and wonder at this great genius. Especially wonder why you've never heard of him.

Have you come across an American pint? It's 500 millilitres instead of 0.56831 though the Americans don't use decimals for most things. That's perhaps because they don't have to worry about Brussels. But I do wish the old system of putting the decimal point in the middle instead of using a full stop had been kept. It made things so much simpler. While I'm blaming the Yanks, do you know that a billion in English used to be a million millions before we gave in to the US and changed ours to a thousand millions?

Now try this one at home: £19 – 19s – 11 ¾d multiplied by eight. See if the youngsters can work it out. If you're anything like my age you can probably see the easiest way of doing it. Any one who went to Prince's Street School will be spot on.

When I was approaching my 70th birthday a friend told me not to worry about 'three score years and ten' being a man's life span. "They've gone decimal," he said, "Start worrying when you get to be 100". Come to think of it, when are we going to turn time into digital?

Days will be the same length and there will still be 365 ¼ of them in a year.

"As the song went, "Rule Britannia, two tanners make a bob; three make eighteen pence and four two bob"

90 YEARS OF PHOTOGRAPHY

Naturally I was not taking photographs in 1923, just being a model, like everyone else's baby. They were all black and white on a box Brownie. There's even a full frontal nude picture of me on holiday at Bournemouth taken when I was about two years old. No, I shan't show you that one, I'm too shy. Mum must have taken them because Dad was always cutting peoples' heads off when he took their pictures. These old photos are somewhere hanging about, either in the spare room or in cupboards or drawers. I am lost in admiration of Allan Frost, who seems to have millions of photographs, all properly documented and organised.

Our family box camera was the sort most people used in the old days. You had to hold it at waist height and peer into a tiny view finder, looking at the subject. There was a small lever on the side of the box, which had to be pressed whilst keeping the camera as still as possible. When you had taken a dozen photos you wound on the film and took it to the chemist, who would develop the negatives and print them on small pieces of glossy paper. Only then did you know what you had actually photographed and it usually was not quite what you meant to do. Oh! How frustrating it all was and relative to income it was expensive too.

Professionals would take pictures of weddings, special events and for newspapers; they also made picture postcards. These were all black and white, though some of them were hand coloured by adding coloured ink to the positive. Sometimes, especially with postcards of exotic places that the photographer didn't know, the results could look rather comical where the wrong colour had been applied. Normally, as now, the professionals took much better pictures than we simple amateurs could do. Of course they charged for this, the price depending on the photographer's reputation.

As you may know, for many years Woolworths had a 3d or 6d price policy but they still managed to sell cheap little cameras for 6d the casing and another 6d for the working parts inside. This may have been a 'loss leader' but they made up for that by selling films and processing them, so that a considerable overall profit ensued. I think the overall cost of using the Woolworth equipment was more than the chemists' charges.

Before the last world War we didn't take many pictures; perhaps there were a dozen or two in a year. Often a special moment was lost because we couldn't find the camera. After the war, in Germany, many of us bought German cameras when we were stationed there in the Army of Occupation. I bought my first, a Zeiss box then. It was an excellent camera too, and took a few pictures, though I rarely remembered to take it with me on trips. There's a good one of the Mohne dam with the sun on the tiny waves.

After leaving the Army I was paid only £125 a year, so living very frugally indeed and unable to afford any photography. It was only when I had a 'proper job' for proper pay that I could take pictures again. I bought a small 127 Kodak camera then, a modern looking instrument that you held up to eye level; that lasted a few years of holiday snaps in black and white.

In 1961 I was elected chairman of the Urban Council, much like the modern Mayor but with far more responsibilities. Wanting to record changes in the town during my year in office I bought an Agfa Silette from Ian McTaggart in Dawley Road and some slide transparency film. Ian wouldn't sell me film until I had played with the camera for a day to get used to it. There are hundreds of slides somewhere of Wellington, our family holidays and pictures for use at Prince's Street School. It was a lovely camera and the coloured slides were often used for lessons until twelve years or more later when it began to falter.

My next camera was a Praktica SLR, an East German make, very reliable, solid and with a shutter that made a loud clang, scaring off wildlife for miles. Sometimes I needed slides and sometimes colour prints, so I had two of them; also I bought a wide-angle lens and a telephoto that fitted either camera. I was feeling very set up as a photographer now. All this equipment was heavy to carry around but great fun to use.

For flash photos we used a strange contraption that fitted on top. It had a fan-like metal mirror throwing the light from a disposable bulb, which had to be replaced for every picture; it was quite a job setting it up, expensive to use and yet another item to be carried. There was no question of automatic exposure or focus, so the old cameras needed to be hand tuned for distance and aperture. You needed to have a light meter as there was none built in, so again another bit of equipment had to go in the bag.

All this gear was in use when I wrote and photographed for my first book in 1987 and several later books. The camera bag, with two Prakticas, three lenses, a 2x extension, light meter, flash contraption, spare bulbs, film and batteries seemed to weigh a ton, especially when hill walking. There was no way I was going to carry a tripod as well, so I bought a monopod which doubled as a walking stick.

Then, just as the Prakticas were wearing out, modern digital cameras became affordable. They are so much easier to use that we all changed, though I was sorry for Alan at the Camera Shop in Walker Street, who lost a lot of trade. Hurrah for the fireworks he sells.

Now most pictures are on phones. Has the fun gone out of photography?

"When you had taken a dozen photos you wound on the film and took it to the chemist, who would develop the negatives and print them on small pieces of glossy paper. Only then did you know what you had actually photographed and it usually was not quite what you meant to do"

FLOOK - MADE IN WELLINGTON

Newspaper cartoons like Thelwell, Giles, Tintin, Asterix and the modern Guardian cartoon 'Clare in the Community' can be brilliantly entertaining. A great one was Flook by Trog in the Daily Mail from 1949 to1984. Long after we had become irritated with the paper's style we continued to take the Daily Mail simply for Flook.

Many readers will remember Rufus, the ginger headed schoolboy and Flook, the creature that came from one of his dreams and accompanied him. Other characters included Douglas Bodger, a ham fisted kind hearted gaolbird-villain, his sister, Lucretia, a witch resembling Lucretia Borgia and 'The Colonel', a retired blimpish officer. The cartoon poked fun at celebrities and especially politicians in a spirit of cheerful irrelevance.

The action took place in a fantasy world. People in the news filled the frames, often with Flook asking the simple questions politicians couldn't possibly answer without getting themselves into dreadful trouble. There was a lot of quite sophisticated satire, with singers, artists, especially those 'famous for being well-known' being gently laughed at.

Wally Fawkes of the jazz group 'Troglodytes' was the artist and signed himself Trog. The script was written by a galaxy of musicians including Humphrey Littleton, George Melly, Barry Took and Barry Norman. No wonder the text was highly intelligent.

'But whatever has this to do with Wellington?' Thank you for being patient enough to get this far without knowing. The answer is that a replica of Flook was made at the Chad Valley works in Orleton Lane, near the railway bridge. This was a little known factory that had taken the place of the Crown Works, where such things as school furniture had been made. Later the works was used by the Pearce family's DIY store and its place has since been taken over for housing.

The factory mainly made rubber ducks of the kind that floated in so many baths. These were made from latex rubber, poured into plaster of Paris moulds and stuffed with kapok. Most had small squeaks in their bottoms. For a few years my father, Eric Evans, was a foreman at the factory. It's not everyone who can say his father worked in a rubber duck factory, but mine certainly did.

Let me explain how the little Flook dolls were made. First a designer made a model; I think it was originally from wood. When the product had been approved by the Chad Valley's board the Orleton Lane works were given the go-ahead. A series of moulds were made from plaster of Paris by pressing the model into the plaster while it was still wet and drying it. The moulds were in two parts, held together by latex bands and had a narrow funnel through which the liquid latex was poured.

The workers poured latex into the mould and baked it in an oven for a short time, then emptied out the latex from the centre, leaving just the 'skin' baked. Spare rubber was kept for re-use. The moulds were put back in the oven for more baking and drying, after which they were dusted with talcum powder, trimmed and stuffed with kapok; later 'squeaks' were inserted and each one painted.

Flooks were made by the dozen, gross and great gross. Most readers will know that a dozen is 12 and some will know a gross is 12 X 12 = 144. But do you know a great gross is 12 x 12 x 12 = 1728? Try asking your friends.

So there's the story of Flook, made in Wellington. Please let us know if you still have one.

08 EVENTS

CHRISTMAS CELEBRATIONS, 1920s AND 1930s

Wrekin News wants a Christmas article; Allan Frost wants one to follow up from his latest book, 'Wellington in the 1920s and 1930s.' All right chaps, you can both have your own way. Never let it be said that I can't rise to a challenge.

Allan's book is full of facts and nostalgia and has many excellent photographs. Although I lived through most of the 20 years he describes, I found it fascinating to be reminded of many things I had forgotten and to learn a few facts that I didn't know about. I can thoroughly recommend it to all, even those whose parents were not born by the time he's writing about. Unfortunately the only bookshop in Wellington is the one in the market but you can get a copy quite easily from Amazon or the publishers, Fonthill Media at Millview House, Toadsmoor Road, Stroud, Gloucestershire (www.fonthillmedia.com)

As I wasn't born until 1923 the first few years will have to remain a blank, but there was a tale my parents told that when I was very little they had decorated the rooms above our shop in High Street after I had been put to bed on Christmas Eve. They had spent a lot of time and trouble putting up streamers, lights, a tree, holly and mistletoe and thought I would be quite delighted with it all. However, for some reason I woke up in a grumpy mood. When they pointed out their decorations, I asked, "Who put all dis wubbish up?" For ever after that all Christmas decorations were referred to as 'wubbish' by the family.

Christmas has changed greatly over the years – like a lot of other things. The idea of celebrating Christmas without going to church used to be thought quite wrong. Nowadays most people seem disinclined to associate the holiday with churches, except for the odd carol. It's now mainly about buying presents and cards and drinks and eating too much turkey, pudding and mince pies.

The one thing that seems to have remained unchanged over the years is that Christmas is especially a time for children. We may have forgotten about the birth of Jesus Christ in many households but then, as now, Christmas was regarded as a family celebration. Even as the TV is blasting out adverts for various people, firms and organisations clamouring to make money out of the festive seasons and the media get excited over trivia and all the trash that has come to be associated, still the most important thing for most of us remains our own families.

In the 1920s there was much less money about and far less advertising of toys and other gifts. Nuts and fruit were the best most children expected. Some lucky kids had fathers who could make toys themselves, mothers who could make dolls' clothes or parents who were rich enough to buy expensive gifts like Meccano sets or Hornby trains. As my dad was in and out of work and some of his jobs were 'commission only', resulting in a big sale occasionally and periods with few sales, our family income varied quite a lot. Even when he had struck a good patch, there was always the memory that the good times may not last so frugality and saving were necessary.

Some things were pretty well guaranteed to happen, many of which are still with us. Holly with berries had to be collected from the hedges and woods, with some ivy and a bit of mistletoe from the market. This must never be put up until Christmas Eve and had to be taken down on 12th night. Why? Because it's bad luck, that's why.

The 1920s saw us trying to get back to the days before the Great War, but then there was an economic disaster and that had to be survived too. By the mid-1930s prosperity was returning and some of the best house-building took place in Wellington, even though the increase in house-buying and consequent mortgages caused some frugal living in Bread-and-Dripping Row and Kippers-and-Curtains Avenue.

One Christmas I had a 'Chemistry Set' which was exciting. You could then buy sulphuric, hydrochloric or nitric acids from the chemist and also iron filings, sulphur and saltpetre to make gunpowder – great fun! I remember mixing hydrogen and oxygen to make water and a very loud bang. Try it now and you'd find yourself a suspected terrorist. Do chemists now sell chemicals at all?

One present I still have is 'The Children's Encyclopaedia' edited by Arthur Mee, which had ten volumes containing thousands of pages of history, geography, biology, philosophy, archaeology, mechanics, art, fables, mathematics, geology, literature, poetry and a miscellaneous collection of Morse code, flags of nations, war medals, military ranks, stamps and everything else that Arthur Mee thought a child should know about. To a lad whose school taught nothing but reading, writing, arithmetic and scripture it was a treasure trove I read often.

To begin with I used to put up a sock at the end of my bed for a hoped-for present but later that changed to a pillowcase. Once there was a small guitar, though I never learned to play it and it didn't last long. Sometimes there were gramophone records, played over and over again on our 'wind-up' portable gramophone.

Nowadays Christmas, for many people, is commercially a huge shopping bonanza when expensive presents are given that often won't last long. Almost everyone is financially much better off than we were in the 1920s and 1930s – yes, really!

But I love it with my large, lovely family. The young ones put up my 'wubbish' and the rest busy themselves keeping everyone else happy, fed and watered.

So there it is, Christmas from 1920 to 1940 and how we are now. Here's wishing all our readers a very merry, happy and peaceful Christmas. Spare a thought for those who are unhappy and do what you can. Then Santa will visit you on Christmas Eve.

"Christmas has changed greatly over the years – like a lot of other things. The idea of celebrating Christmas without going to church used to be thought quite wrong"

THE GHOSTS OF CHRISTMAS PAST

The first Christmas I have any memory of was in 1927 when we lived over the shop at 49 High Street. Mainly I remember the tale my parents told often and this is it... Apparently they had spent ages putting up decorations while I was in bed fast asleep. In the morning, for some reason, I woke up grumpily, looked at the tinsel and streamers and demanded, "Who put this rubbish up?" They were not best pleased, but they said when I had properly woken up I was as excited as any four year old should be.

Over the years there have been some quite varied Christmas Days and as I write now I'm looking forward to Christmas Day 2012 with some of my family in Much Wenlock and hope to see them all over the holiday period, somewhere, some time. For me, as I suppose most people, this is a family occasion, whether or not it has religious significance.

In the early 1930s my Dad was out of work, scratting a living selling paint, water softeners or batteries and doing anything to earn a bob or two, so money was very short. However, we managed to enjoy ourselves in a frugal way. Still some decorations (always called 'rubbish') went up on Christmas Eve, though never a moment before; putting them up too soon was reckoned to be bad luck. Nobody seemed to know why. Of course there had to be holly, as there is still. We never had any alcohol at Christmas or any other time because we were teetotallers and Rechabites. Mince pies and Christmas pudding were my favourites and still are. We always went to church or chapel on Christmas Day.

In the Army between 1942 and 1946 it was Army Christmas, with a decorated mess hall and being served by the sergeants, Warrant Officers and officers. Army cooks always managed to save something from the rations to make Christmas special. However, 1944 was spent in trenches beside the River Maas, with ice floating down the river. Across the river were Germans, occasionally plastering our positions with rockets from their 'Moaning Minnie'. We usually replied with machine gun fire or mortars. But for Christmas Day neither side fired, though I'm pretty sure there was no communication between them. We had a rum ration. Later I met one of the Germans, who told the same tale from his side.

In 1945 we were in Flensburg, Schleswig-Holstein, where the Angles came from, and invited the local Infants' School for Christmas tea. The kids were scared of us but soon began to enjoy themselves when the Sergeant Major picked one of them up and galloped round the room. They drank 'pop' and ate sandwiches and cakes until they were full, so after singing 'Stille Nacht' for us they went home with doggy bags. I was amazed that the Army had done something right.

Back home for 1946 and things were in short supply. My civilian rations were not as much as they had been in the Army, nor was my pay. I'd been getting 10s 6d per day and all my keep; now it was a struggle to live in lodgings on £125 per year – that's £75 a year less and everything to be paid for. Fortunately my parents supported me and I had saved, though it was over three years before I was paid enough to live on as a qualified teacher.

Even then life was frugal and Christmas presents had to be cheap. Fortunately the children had a full set of grandparents who were more generous than we could afford to be.

Christmas at Prince's Street School was a huge effort. There were carols, cards, decorations, parties, games, jelly, mixed with exams and reports. It was murder. I was completely exhausted by the time we broke up and had to start on my own family.

Gradually, over the years I've watched our children grow up, marry, and have children of their own. One year two grandchildren were staying with us over Christmas Eve. When Santa called they were fast asleep (well they seemed to be) and they had been reasonably good most of the year, so their spare pillowcases were filled with presents. No sooner had we climbed into bed than there were little rustlings in the next room. Excited words were whispered. Paper was torn. Lots of giggling, muttering and wriggling went on – for too long. We were finding it difficult to sleep so I let out a stentorian, teacherish bellow and the noise subsided long enough for us to nod off. Kids – who'd have 'em? Well, me for one, despite their disadvantages.

As the years went by life became easier but our frugal habits have continued. We've kept last year's decorations and now great-grandchildren festoon the tree for me. A few years ago, finding it was hard work hunting berried holly, I bought some variegated holly plants so I use my own from the garden. This year, as usual, I'm invited to Much Wenlock and have promised to take the brandy butter for the pudding. The days of teetotalism have long gone. I'm hoping to see all my family and their partners at some time over the Christmas period.

Although most of us don't go to church there are lots of Christian traditions we still enjoy, like Carols, some of which have beautiful music. Unfortunately I can't sing in tune but that doesn't stop me enjoying the carols. Some years we used to sing with some local patients and I wrote a Mumming Play for them.

Christmas gets longer each year. It used to start at Advent; now the mince pies begin before Easter eggs. Decorating started at Christmas Eve; now it's Midsummer.

This year I'll stuff myself with pies and puddings and cakes washed down with a drop of wine – then go and sleep it off. Isn't life terrible for us poor old pensioners?

Thank God for kids. Merry Christmas.

"We usually replied with machine gun fire or mortars. But for Christmas Day neither side fired, though I'm pretty sure there was no communication between them. We had a rum ration. Later I met one of the Germans, who told the same tale from his side"

OSWALD MOSLEY AND THE WELLINGTON RIOT

Some time before the Last World War we had a large and exciting riot in Wellington. At the time I was a lad at the High School; not a teenager, because the word had not been imported from America, but a lad. I must have been about 15 or 16. I'd had an early growth-spurt, so I was a man-sized boy who shaved and smoked a pipe.

For a couple of years I had corresponded with 'pen-pals' in several countries, especially those surrounding the Third Reich. This was a bit like Facebook. There were writers in Belgium, Netherlands, Denmark, Poland, Czecho-Slovakia, Austria and France. We exchanged news and views about the world especially our own way of life and concerns for the future. It was an offshoot of my continuing interest in (or obsession with) geography.

We had heard about Sir Oswald Mosley and his British Union of Fascists because my family took the Daily Mail, which had supported him. My friend, Bill Evans (no relation) and I decided we had to go and see this meeting that the Wellington Journal said would take place in the Market Square on the Saturday. It might be fun, we thought.

We knew that Mosley had been a Member of Parliament, successively Conservative, Independent and Labour; also that he had at one time been part of a Labour Government but resigned. We knew that he was related to several aristocrats and had many friends in High Places and was an admirer of Adolf Hitler and Benito Mussolini. He struck us as an interesting nutcase who might be entertaining. We had also heard that the Dawley, Madeley and Oakengates miners had been influenced by Communists in their unions and were going to turn up in opposition. "What FUN!" We thought, "let's go!"

Bill and I met in Market Square some time before the event. Bill's father, Jack Evans, was the local police Inspector and he was marshalling his 'troops'. He insisted in locking Bill in the entrance to Hobsons' shop; they had an iron gate across the entrance, where the travel shop is now. I declined his offer, preferring to be free to run away should the violence he expected break out. All the shops were closed and locked.

There was a small crowd gathering, curious to know what would happen. Mosley's small car was in front of No. 1 (now occupied by Subway) and loudspeakers were being attached to a framework on the top. The Fascists marched down New Street and surrounded the car. I don't remember them being as many as the Chief Constable's report says; more like a dozen or two it seems, though perhaps he was right. There were several black-shirted 'minders' with folded arms and grim expressions surrounding Mosley.

Then the miners came up from the railway station. They were a tough looking bunch too, but much more cheerful. I decided to melt in with the miners. The Square filled with men. Someone (perhaps a PR man or assistant) introduced Mosley in a 'posh' voice, praising him as a great leader or something like that. As soon as Mosley began to speak he was drowned by shouting miners, so I have no idea what he said. The loud speakers couldn't compete with several hundred miners.

The shop girls from JC Lloyd's grocers shop, (where Britannia/Co-op is now) opened the upstairs window and began throwing out-dated eggs, tomatoes and cabbages at the Blackshirts, which was good fun. One of the girls was Bill's sister.

For some time the shouting went on, Mosley trying to make his speech and the miners – and the rest of us too – drowning him out. I can't remember what was shouted but I think there were chants, perhaps led by Communists or miners' leaders, which may have been the same thing. There was Mosley, shouting at his microphone by the car, surrounded by his thugs, then a small space, then a thin row of policemen, then a dense crowd of yelling protesters stretching back from the Square and up Church Street. Perhaps there were more on the south side of the Square and up New Street but I couldn't see them.

Nobody was armed; the policemen had their truncheons but didn't draw them, probably on orders from Inspector Jack Evans. There were no missiles apart from the fruit and vegetables. Gradually the crowd began to get more excited and threatening. For a time there seemed to be a lot of lurching backwards and forwards. The police, although heavily outnumbered, were not seen to be the enemy and for a time held the crowd back simply by their presence and the respect we all had for them.

Eventually the crowd broke through the police cordon by sheer weight of numbers, pushing them aside. I heard a story that one policeman, a chap named McMahon, a big 18 stone man, was picked up and passed back overhead by the crowd, finally being put down gently at the back. It may not be true but it was a good story. By this time I had worked my way from the middle to the back of the crowd, about where the Town Clock used to be. Things were getting rough and I didn't want to get hurt; my survival instinct has always been strong

A few Blackshirts were pushing their way through the crowd, being slapped and punched all the way. They were trying to get down Market Street and I confess to thumping one as he passed. That was my first blow for freedom, or so I thought.

Eventually the crowd broke up and everyone went home. I was told that the big window at the Cock Hotel, where Mosley was staying, was broken when someone threw a brick at him; that may be true. Back at school we went round giving Nazi salutes and shouting, "Heil Ossie" which seemed fun.

That's what I remember, after over 70 years; accuracy isn't guaranteed.

"They were trying to get down Market Street and I confess to thumping one as he passed. That was my first blow for freedom, or so I thought"

TWO FOR THE PRICE OF ONE

PEACE AND LITERATURE

Often I'm stopped in the street and asked for permission to plant something in Wellington's new Peace Garden. I explain that there are no rules and everyone is trusted to do what they think is right. It's not my garden; it belongs to all Wellington people. So if you are sure about it, do it. There's a group of volunteers, chaired by Helen King, who will give advice if you ask them. They look after the garden very well.

Our garden is a long narrow strip opposite the new Civic Centre. It has cost the taxpayers nothing as the Borough Council simply allowed us to plant a Peace Garden on a patch of land that couldn't be otherwise used. Most of the plants so far have been bought by individuals locally; some have simply come from their own gardens.

Some folks are planting in memory of a loved one; my family planted for Naomi, my late wife, their mother, grandmother and great grandmother. Some, like Lions and Germans, are planting to show that they support peace and are against all wars, or to make a statement on behalf of their organisations. Many plants are there simply to make the town look beautiful.

We would very much like more support from our schools. We'd like to see all the schools and colleges in and around the town using the garden to plant flowers or to string up peace messages. Of course we will come round to help and talk if needed. Who will be first?

Religious people are welcome too – all of them. Quakers have led the way. Christians, Muslims, Sikhs, Hindus and Buddhists are all in favour of peace (theoretically at least) and welcome to join in the garden. This invitation is open to peaceful Atheists and Agnostics too of course. Let's hope nobody wants to fight about who is the most peaceful!

Victims of war should surely be commemorated, including the wounded who survived, so having no place on war memorials. Both my parents suffered from the Great War in 1917; I intend to plant for them. Many survivors gave years of their lives for their country yet there is no memorial to them. There could be here, in our Peace Garden if you wish; it's up to us.

Our last Mass Planting session on 28th April was a great success so we're having another on 15th September. The team will be there with wise advice, I'll have labels if needed and everyone is welcome. Do please join in and plant for whatever peaceful reason you think fit.

There's no need to wait for 15th and no reason not to do your planting on your own at any time but we are hoping for a good crowd on the day and it will be a friendly occasion.

Plant for peace – do it soon.

NOW FOR OUR WONDERFUL LITERARY FESTIVAL

Pat Fairclough, chairman of the Festival committee, is excited about this year's programme. You can get one from our lovely new library or from the information desk. We have the biggest and best FREE Literary Festival in England – did you know that?

Years ago, when we were inventing the festival it seemed we had a good idea and it's a delight to watch it grow. Local writers group Wrekin Writers run their annual Writers' Workshop as they have since the beginning but as usual there are new events this year. They organise their own course and it's not free but it's highly recommended and usually brilliant. Some events are in the new library, others at Wrekin, New and Telford Colleges, also the Old Orleton and William Withering. There's no room here for the whole programme, so do pick one up and see. They are available at the library and Civic Centre – free of course.

The programme is aimed to include something for everyone, so few will like everything and very few will not find something to their taste. Most people will enjoy many events, so you will have to pick those you fancy. Some of the most popular are usually booked up so apply for tickets early.

Pat Fairclough has asked me to highlight a few of the best, including Rachel Crowther's Stories and Secrets, Catherine Cooper and Mollie Bolt's Poetry Trail, Ted Cowling, fun poet Aiden Flynn in the William Withering and Wellington Walkers' Walking Festival. Olwen Marmion and Kate Boulter now run the Peggie Harrison children's poetry competition and winning entries will be displayed in the library. There's a Dickens of a lot about Dickens this year including the brilliant Geoff Hales.

Most popular (tickets required) include Bob Flowerdew and Josceline Dimbleby, and my guess is that Wellington historian Allan Frost's talk called Made in Wellington will be full too. Many younger Wellingtonians don't know that within living memory (mine at least) this was a prominent manufacturing town. In fact he may be more popular than the expensively imported speakers.

There are three sessions in the library with local authors (well, some of them) which enable our local talent to show off their latest books and perhaps tell you what they will be writing next. It's well worthwhile going along and maybe buying their latest.

One thing missing this year, as last year, is the Black History Month celebration of the stories of colourful locals whose origins are far away. Their personal histories make fascinating reading; I just hope something appears next year. Incidentally we'd have had far fewer Olympic medals had we been restricted to Anglo-Saxon-Celt competitors.

However, Wellington Literary Festival is a series of events well worth supporting and it's worth while getting a programme soon and deciding which events suit you, your family and friends. This is something Wellington shines at, so join in and be a part of the biggest and best in Britain. You'll be glad you did.

09 PLACES

WELLINGTON CEMETERY

It's a peaceful place, our town cemetery. It's also very interesting if you look carefully at the gravestones; more so if you know a bit of the town's history or have a long memory. Lately I have taken to walking around there, mainly because walking is the best exercise you can get and I have needed to do a lot of that to get back to health again. Contrary to what some folks may think, there's nothing at all morbid in a gentle stroll around the well-kept graves and occasional trees with their birds and squirrels.

The area is dominated by the two semi-detached chapels and their communal spire. It's a very pleasant building and a great pity that, apart from tool storage, the chapels are unused. Some years back it was falling into decay due to neglect; some of us worried that it would disintegrate altogether. There were blocked pipes and drains, water was getting in through the roof, spoiling the plaster; grass and small trees grew from the guttering. If this had continued we felt, a fine building would become a ruin.

Wellington Civic Society wrote to Wrekin Council, who owned it, complaining about its sad state, praising its design and asking for their help. We grumbled and begged, at first with little reply. There was no money for repair and the building was no longer used; perhaps it should be demolished. We were horrified and started a campaign in the press and on radio. Attention began to be paid and local friends joined in with our protests. Then a cremation firm became interested; they thought it might make a good crematorium. We became excited about this prospect and promoted the idea but it failed because of health regulations specifying the distance a crematorium must be from houses. The idea became unfeasible. Eventually Red Hill was chosen as the site, which has been a great success.

Long ago the chapels were well used. One was for Methodists, the other for the Church of England. Roman Catholics had to use the archway between the two for their services. In those days religions other than Christian were quite unknown here. Nowadays of course services are performed in the appropriate church, mosque, gurdwara or wherever the person worshipped or else, and increasingly, at the crematorium. There are, however, areas set for specific religions and denominations of Christianity. The latest is a Muslim section, where I was interested to see names of friends I had known well. Appropriately their graves are aligned towards Mecca.

When it was first opened, Wellington was so proud of the new cemetery that the bottom of Haygate Road as well as Linden Avenue was named Cemetery Road. This is still the main entrance, though it can also be approached via Union Road, by a footpath (sadly needing resurfacing) from Holyhead Road and also from Bowring Park.

Coming in from Linden Avenue, through the main entrance, the first big grave on the left it that of the family of Owen Downey Murphy, the brewer, 'pop' maker and owner of pubs for many miles around. Many years ago 'OD' came to Coalbrookdale; he made 'pop' in his kitchen and sold it from a horse-drawn cart. He worked hard, prospered and moved his business to the warehouse (now a museum) in Ironbridge. When a Wellington brewer was selling his brewery on condition no beer was brewed there he took it over as a mineral water works from which he expanded. The grave includes his sons, Ronald and Graham who were UDC councillors in the 1950s. I remember asking Graham how to make money, as I was feeling rather poor at the time and he was quite wealthy. "It helps if your father leaves you a brewery," he replied. The two businesses, Wrekin

Brewery Co. and OD Murphy and Sons were sold to Greenall Whitley, who themselves were bought up and closed. I think it's called asset stripping.

Further on is a tall obelisk erected to remember another Victorian who became wealthy – Richard Groom. Richard was a basket maker in High Street, who saw the possibility of using the large factory that had been set up to manufacture stations, carriages, signal boxes and all things necessary for the railway when it came in 1849. He turned Shropshire Works into one of the largest timber businesses in Britain and also worked to improve local schools and the Methodist Church. Richard bought Dothill, the home of the Lords Forester after they moved to Willey Park. Nothing remains of this large factory now except the name, 'Groom's Alley'.

There's an elaborate gravestone to the Hyatt family. Mrs Hyatt was the founder of Hyatt's Ladies College, which continued to be a private girls' secondary school long after she died. When the intake to the Shropshire County Council run Wellington Girls' High School was increased the roll numbers fell and Hyatt's finally closed.

These three graves remind me of the poem, 'Ozymandias', which tells of the crumbling remains of a huge statue in the desert. The inscription below it says, "My name is Ozymandias, King of Kings. Look on my works, ye mighty and despair". There's nothing else there.

Tucked away in the middle of the old Methodist section (there seems not to be a Methodist area in the new extension) is a double grave surrounded by a low white kerb. It's dedicated to Thomas Hall Fail and Drusilla Emily Fail. Drusilla died in 1917 and Thomas in 1940. They were my grandparents. Of course I never met Drusilla but Thomas lived with us and I remember him well as a kind grandfather and a strict Rechabite teetotaller who had been a railway signalman after serving in the Army. Like the rest of my family he never had much money.

Wellington Cemetery is looked after by the Borough Council and they seem to do a good job. It's a pleasant place for a quiet walk, full of interest to anyone who respects the town's past.

"Contrary to what some folks may think, there's nothing at all morbid in a gentle stroll around the well-kept graves and occasional trees with their birds and squirrels"

SUNNYCROFT

Some years ago I wrote about this newly opened National Trust house in Wellington hoping that more local people would come around to look at it and indeed they did. Since then many things have changed at Sunnycroft; it's much more accessible and a great deal more attractive.

At first you had to park in Wrekin Road and walk up Highfield Alley; now there's free parking for around 30 cars. Life is easier now we locals and the volunteers have been listened to. The emphasis was on the house being a 'Gentleman's Residence' as a building; now Joan Lander, the needlework genius who gave the house to the Trust is being recognised for her achievements and wonderful work together with the fascination of seeing how the Landers, a well-heeled local family, lived in their days.

Earlier it was a great struggle to attract volunteers to work in the house and gardens; now around 120 volunteers are happily busy. The car park is often full so it would be a good thing for those of us who live nearby to walk – good for our health too. The gardens, neglected for so long, are coming to life, thanks to Joel the gardener and his friendly helpers. Sunnycroft is a great credit to those who work there and also to Wellington. We should take pride in our origins and support the efforts that are made for us.

Claire Reeves is the latest 'Lady in Charge' (Her proper title is 'House and Visitor Service Manager) She's charming, a great enthusiast and full of ideas, a great advantage when dealing with the volunteers, without whom the place wouldn't function. If she wasn't so keen they wouldn't be there. Between them, Claire and the rest have vastly improved the whole ambience. It's changed from a moderately interesting history lesson to a good time out, with lots of things to see and do.

The gardens too have changed, mainly through the efforts of Joel and his group of volunteers, who have planted flowers, fruit trees and vegetables, now sold from the allotments when they're in season. He leads groups round the garden (12.30 & 3pm) and there are bowls and croquet games on the big lawn. Joel is well worth listening to, 'a sage who knows his onions'. A gentle potter round the gardens with him is both a delight and instructive. The large old glasshouse is a fascination in itself. There's a reception hut in the car park at the front with visitor lavatories and a book shop in the courtyard at the back. Traditional teas and cakes are provided – pricey but delicious, and served in the house or out on the veranda.

Sunnycroft at first seems hidden away behind a huge hedge on Holyhead Road. The approach to the house is down a drive with an avenue with enormous Wellingtonias towering above, curving left into an open space before the front door of the house. Tickets for the house tours are obtained from the reception hut in the car park. Indoors is the entrance hall with its elegant staircase, where you are met by your guide and shown round. The guides are all volunteers and most knowledgeable about the house and its earlier inhabitants, bubbling over with enthusiasm. It's fascinating to glimpse a way of life that was comfortable, affluent and so very different in many ways from our own. Many little things are displayed, giving a taste of the intimate details of Edwardian times. The Landers didn't like waste, so these have been kept in the house until it was given to the National Trust by its last owner, Joan Lander.

Some years ago, before the National Trust took over, my wife organised a charity party at Sunnycroft with the help of Joan Lander. She allowed some rooms to be used for the party and I remember noticing that wartime blackout curtains were still at the windows, at least fifty years after the war. Nothing was thrown away if there was any chance it might 'come in useful'. New visitors will be amazed at the collection of medicines kept in a cupboard and especially at the collection of scents wafting from it.

Cows were kept in the field that is now Rose Crescent and the milk was sold to local people, who brought their own jugs to be filled from the churn using a ladle. Spare fruit and vegetables from the gardens and eggs were sold too.

In the exhibition room are displays of Joan Lander's wonderful needlework, her fascinating patterns, embroidery and beadwork, including some by 'Granny Hunt'. Many will feel that the needlework alone is well worth a visit.

The house seems happier now, with all its visitors and volunteers than ever it was when it was a family home, though they used to have occasional parties for their friends – mostly the town's elite and prosperous. Claire tells me that there were almost 15,000 visitors last year and she expects there will be more than that this year. No wonder the Maws tiles in the entrance hall need conservation.

There must be many Wellingtonians who haven't been to Sunnycroft yet; I can't emphasise enough what an enjoyable visit it has now become and urge you all to go and see for yourselves this wonderful little gem on our doorsteps. If you went some time ago, there's much more to see now.

"Claire tells me that there were almost 15,000 visitors last year and she expects there will be more than that this year. No wonder the Maws tiles in the entrance hall need conservation"

DOTHILL - THE DAY I BOUGHT AN ESTATE!

One day in 1961, while I was chairman of Wellington Urban District Council, I had a message from Reuben Rushen, the Town Clerk that he wanted to see me in his office as soon as possible. He had before him the many sheets of paper that made up the conveyance document, transferring the ownership of the whole Dothill estate to the council. This was the final part of the takeover of the land by the council and it needed the chairman's signature and the council's seal of office to complete the legal procedure.

Reuben explained the whole process and witnessed my signature on a document involving far more money than I had ever dreamed of. Then he heated sealing wax, dropped a blob on the paper and set up the small press that applied the official UDC seal. The council had negotiated this sale several years ago – and had actually owned the land since 1956 – all we were doing was putting the finishing touches to an arrangement that had been long agreed.

The vendor was Harry Hodgson, a Canadian, who was the Managing Director of Joseph Sankey and Sons of Hadley Castle Works. He sold it to the council as 'agricultural land', at a much lower price than if there had there been planning permission for the housing and development we were intending. Not only the treasurer, Ollie Leighton, but also the two councillors who were chartered accountants, Sidney Parker and Graham Murphy, assured us that this was an excellent deal and I'm sure they were right.

Dothill was one of Wellington's 'berewicks' at Domesday, nearly 1,000 years ago. Giles of Erdington, lord of Wellington, (who obtained the market charter in 1244) leased it to John de Praéres for the service of one sixth of a knight's service. Lord Forester owned it for some time, until by 1922 it was owned by Ernest Groom (the great timber merchant, remembered in Grooms Alley). Later ownership passed to HF Hodgson mentioned above. He sold 197 acres and the house to Wellington UDC in 1956, by which time I remember him living at Hadley Park House. He later built a house in Lilleshall, called 'Hi'.

During the Last World War Dothill, like Admaston, was defended against all enemies by the Home Guard and I well remember roaming over the fields and round the pools on duty or exercises. Don't laugh too loudly at my Dad's little army – at least they kept all the Nazi hordes from invading Wellington throughout the War without hurting anyone. In those days a man we called 'Jock' (I never knew his proper name) farmed the land.

By the time I signed the conveyance the UDC had many plans for Dothill and so had Shropshire County Council, including Park Junior School, St' Patrick's Primary School, Dothill Infants and Junior Schools and the Girls' Secondary Modern School. Also we had built the houses on North Road and what was then Hawkstone Court and Haughmond Court, the tall blocks of flats.

Part of the land was sold to the Shrewsbury firm of Fletcher Estates, which began planning and building many houses and the local shops. The money from Fletchers paid for the rest of the land, as it was so very much more valuable with planning permission for building than it had been when we bought it as 'agricultural' land. This is the secret of the financing of Telford – buying agricultural land and selling it as building land brings in a huge profit.

Many new street names were needed and the UDC was looking for a whole lot of suitable names. As chairman of the planning committee I was asked to make out a list and sat down with the Ordnance Survey maps of Shropshire, noting suitable river and stream names, followed by village names. So if residents of the Dothill area don't like their addresses, they should blame me.

The north part of Dothill could not be developed until the Sewage Works had been moved, as there would not have been sufficient 'fall' for the sewers to operate. This happened much later and the names there are not attributable to me. Severn Drive was intended to be much longer but someone decided it had to be cut in two; otherwise it would have been much easier to get to Shawbirch from Wellington Town Centre than it is now. That, I think, was a mistake, causing some Shawbirch people to consider themselves not part of Wellington town.

During my lifetime Dothill, previously the residence and estate of the Lords Forester, has changed from a large farming area to what seems a comfortable, reasonably well planned part of Wellington. House prices reflect the view that it is a pleasant place to live.

BRINGING THE CLIFTON BACK TO LIFE

Oh the nostalgia! So many of us remember the old Clifton don't we? Some of us were there when Major 'Teddy' Herbert of Orleton, later Earl of Powis, opened it in1937 and joined in the 30,000 strong petition in 1983 to keep it going. If you have records or photos of happy memories the Clifton Community Arts Centre team would be interested in them.

Mind if I have a little reminisce first? As a teenager I took my very first girlfriend to the Clifton, though she had to pay for herself as I had no money. Being naïve I didn't understand why she wanted to sit on the back row. Much later, as Chairman of the Road Safety Committee, I wanted to publicise Cycling Proficiency and stood on the stage between films at the Saturday Matinee. The acoustics were wonderful; about a thousand children heard clearly when I spoke in a normal classroom voice.

But now let's get down to a bit of proper history with the help of Dave Weston, whose informative article on the Clifton's History has been sent me by Bill Graham, Venue and Design Consultant

We've had four cinemas in Wellington; the Picture Pavilion in Mill Bank, the Grand Cinema in Tan Bank, the Town Hall in Market Street and the Clifton. The Pavilion was short lived and the Town Hall occasionally called the Bug Hutch. The Grand, originally a skating rink and the Clifton were the posh ones.

Going to the pictures was the thing to do and the Clifton was the most popular for miles around. Many of the best films were able to transport us from our day to day lives into a fantasy world. Especially during wartime this was so and forces people used to fill the place. It was, to use a much-misused word correctly, fantastic.

It was fun to watch the faces of people coming out and guess what sort of film they had seen. If there had been a car chase it was safer to stay away until the demon drivers had gone home and girls who had just seen a 'weepy' were easy to chat up unless with their boyfriends.

There were also news programmes and I well remember some early wartime ones before the

Army got me, the Coronation and the ascent of Everest.

Gradually they all closed, mainly I think because everyone stayed at home to watch TV after that became popular in the late '50s, increasing to the '80s. Then Telford decided to build a multi-screen place and that seemed to frighten the owners off. This was when the Development Corporation were deliberately trying to take everything from the towns within their Development Area and concentrate it in the misnamed Town Centre.

There was a while when a few 'dodgy' films were shown, (or so I was told, though I didn't go then) and a strange idea called Laser Quest that I didn't understand. Next came Saverite, followed by Dunelm; now there's nothing but an empty shell, our memories and hopes and a group of dynamic businessmen with what seems to me a pretty shrewd plan for something quite wonderful.

This is Bill Graham, Fiona Hunter and friends; they certainly impress me. Have a look on www.theclifton.org if you have a computer, or ask someone to look it up for you. See what you think. My first reaction to news in the press was that their ideas were pie in the sky, quite impossible and unattainable. "Fat chance", I said, but I have changed my mind. Not only do they have some wonderful ideas but they have worked out a practical, businesslike way of getting what they – and we – want.

There is no chance of a thousand-seater cinema, like the old Clifton used to be, in these days of television and computer entertainment. It just wouldn't work and the owners would fare no better than they did in the 1980s.

So what is being proposed? Actually it is something both in tune with the modern world and a better deal than bringing back the old days.

First a lot of repairs have to be done. There's the odd leak due to weather and old age and also due to the various alterations made by the laser chaps, Saverite and Dunelm, though the outside seems mainly to be still in good condition.

Then the building needs to be adapted for its new uses. What will it create? The best way I can tell it is to quote what Bill Graham sent me, so here it is:

1. A fully flexible, community led, co-operatively owned but professionally managed Community Arts Centre, accessible and available to all sections of the community.
2. A series of multi-purpose spaces tailored for use by community groups, activity providers, musicians, performers, multi-media activities, skills tuition and local businesses.
3. Workshop, display and educational spaces for local craftspeople.
4. Exhibition areas for local artists, photographers and historians
5. A 100 seat digital cinema.
6. A 400 seat flexible auditorium for performances, drama and ballroom dancing.
7. An arts-themed café bar with free internet access.
8. A high class public access facility, open seven days and 80 hours a week.

There now – there must be something in that for you, whatever your age and background. Schools and colleges will use it; clubs and societies, professional entertainers of all sorts, and of course it'll be a good place for an evening out for everyone within range. This isn't just for Wellington it's for everyone in the area.

So, if you want THE CLIFTON COMMUNITY ARTS CENTRE, tell everyone. The steering group would like your memories and photographs and programmes. They need your support and they need it now. They need to be able to prove to the grant providers and public bodies that they have public support. They need evidence of our support and future use of the Clifton to prove their point. Do everything you can to help them.

10 AND FINALLY A FEW FAVOURITES

THE HISTORY OF A HOUSE
42/44 ROSEWAY, WELLINGTON 1954-1964

I have called the house 42/44 because when I bought it the number was 42 but when I sold it the council had changed the number to 44. The dates may be a year or two out, this is from memory.

This little story is of the first ten years or so of a house in which my family and I lived very happily. I hope it will stimulate other people to write the stories of their houses.

When we were married in 1950 there was a housing shortage due, of course, to the Last World War. There had been some house building in Wellington but it was reserved for the workers at Donnington Ordnance Depot, who had been moved from Woolwich. For ordinary people like us there was almost no accommodation, except when the Urban District Council began to build estates at Arleston. These houses, however, were reserved for people with bigger problems than we had, such as really gross overcrowding. The allocation of council houses was on a strict 'points' basis. You could get points for children and for having to live in really dire circumstances. We could have lived with either of our parents but didn't want to.

We applied for a council house but the waiting list was very long, so we began married life in Greenacres, Ketley Bank, renting a bedroom, sitting room and shared use of the kitchen and bathroom. Then we moved to a flat above two shops in New Street (it's now in High Street). When our first son was born we had a few more points but were still a long way from getting a council house.

Then we heard that Fletcher Estates, jointly with the Council, were about to build six houses in Roseway for sale. We 'phoned Fletchers who said they could only sell to people on the council lists and there were a hundred people waiting. Later we heard that Fletchers had offered houses to people on the top of the list, who had refused and were getting fed up with this. I phoned again and was told to come and talk.

The price was £1,995 each house; £100 deposit, the rest on a fixed mortgage at 4% for 30 years. We picked a pair, paid the deposit and went home to wait for the houses to be built. It was going to cost more than council rents but not that much more; we could only just afford it but at least it would be ours in thirty years' time. Building soon started and we watched the 'footings' being laid out by the light of the gas street lamp outside. This was very exciting.

On one visit I saw a brick wall upstairs being built and worried that there was no wall to hold it up. After a restless night I peered at it in the morning and found it was supported by a steel girder. I felt stupid but relieved. We became friends with the foreman and asked if we could move in during August, which, after several delays and panics, we did. Thus we became Fletcher's first post-war Wellington customer.

We settled in with our neighbours and put a gate in the fence between us at the back, also left the front garden unfenced agreeing to cut the shared front lawn alternately. Soon there was another mouth to feed as our second son appeared so we decided that was a big enough family. Money was in short supply and every penny had to be watched as there was only my small salary to live on, but we had a lot of help from both our families and were very happy there.

Gradually we made sense of the garden, which sloped steeply down to Culvert Alley at the back and had several tall trees. A rope and a board made a swing for the boys and we made a path down to the bottom with plants and shrubs and a small lawn on the flattish bit near the house. Because I like house names, I called it 'Priorswood'. On an old map there was a small wood around there and it belonged to a house called The Priory, though I later discovered it was an old vicarage that had been sold and the new owners had called it The Priory. Then the whole area became called The Priory Estate.

Inside the walls had been painted. We wanted to wallpaper some of them but had to wait until they dried out. Our first attempt was some green paper on the chimney breast and it didn't take long to discover that neither of us was good at papering. Later, attempting a ceiling, I was putting the paper on while my wife held it; it came tumbling down and wrapped round her neck. When I was nailing some floor covering down I kept hitting my thumb; our elder son said, "Daddy 'Blast it'", some of the first words he learned. I was glad when later on we could afford to have Jim Elphick from across the road to decorate.

We had many parties in that house and a lot of fun. I used to sit the children on the side retainer wall to photograph birthday parties. We planted a peach tree in the front garden. First it had no fruit but the year we left it had 365 peaches. The window frames were steel and the tiles were concrete because of the shortage of building materials. The only heating was a coal fire in the sitting room, otherwise we had electric heaters.

We all enjoyed that first house, where we lived for about ten years before moving to 3 Priory Close – just round the corner. I do hope the present occupiers are as happy there as we were.

EARLY INDUSTRIAL ARCHAEOLOGY IN IRONBRIDGE

Some time ago I heard talk that the Ironbridge Gorge was the ancient historic part of Shropshire. Laughingly I suggested that Wellington had been a town for at least half a millennium before anybody thought of building a bridge out of iron and fifty years ago nobody much had heard of this bridge.

Around half a century ago a course was arranged jointly by Birmingham University, the Workers' Education Association and the Youth Hostels Association to study the industrial archaeology of the Ironbridge Gorge and incorporating a short visit to Shrewsbury. The leader was Michael Rix, who had a strong claim to be the inventor of industrial archaeology and was sure that he had been the first person to use the expression in a book. I have often wondered if this was where the idea of the Ironbridge Gorge Museum was born.

In those days few people ever thought of archaeology as including the early industrial history, regarding it as confined to very ancient times, especially pre-history. Most thought the expression 'Industrial Archaeology' was an oxymoron. The study is now well accepted, as is the concept of the Ironbridge Gorge area. Then there was no thought of the present day museum or of the World Heritage Site.

Michael was a tutor at Birmingham and the leader of the course; I was invited to be his assistant and a sort of 'legs man', and to lead walks for him, especially in the gorge. Quite often we became a sort of cross-talk act, where he was the academic and I was adding bits of local information. For instance when we went to see Blists' Hill I contributed the fact that locals called the area Blesses' Hill and the road outside it was Dabberly Lane.

We started our perambulations in Coalbrookdale with a visit to the small museum, now long gone, which had been set up by the Coalbrookdale Company to celebrate their centenary, in a wooden shed where the car park for the museum of iron is now. It was kept by a Mr Timmins, and I had taken children there, so knew it well. We went on to the old furnace that pre-dated Abraham Darby's experiments in 1709 to use coke as the fuel for iron founding.

Then we walked down to the river, the warehouse and the iron bridge. I added a little post-glacial geology and asked the students to 'stand heavy' in the middle of the bridge while explaining that the rocks on each side were trying to bend the bridge and they were standing just where it would eventually fracture. Also I asked, as I still do, just how the bridge was erected over the busy river.

Walking down the river, past the few shops we saw some walls constructed of furnace slag and the overgrown Bedlam Furnace. Most of the old workmen's cottages were still there and there were more small shops, more pubs and virtually no cafés. Many houses and gardens were neglected and overgrown and there was a considerable air of poverty, unlike the 'gentrified' touristy atmosphere now.

On we went, past the concrete Free Bridge, along roads in need of widening and surfacing to the inclined plane, the canal and tar tunnel to Coalport. Michael turned up often, offering pearls of wisdom and advice; he was not physically well enough to do the walk but had plenty of enthusiasm. We studied the bottle kilns and the workshops where the painting and processing had taken place. The only work there at the time was the making of mats from old rubber tyres, otherwise there was a lot of neglect. I added a little about my wife's aunt, who painted some of the Coalport china as a young girl and remembered the stench of burning bones across the road. Bones were added to the kaolin to make bone china. That was before the 1920s strike, after which the firm relocated to the potteries.

Particularly impressive was the standard of the students on this course and the discussions over meals in the hostel and on the walks. Some were talking knowledgably about 'web offset' printing and I learned that they were going to set up a printing works at Ketley for the new Shropshire Star. Others talked of the need for a museum of some kind, probably in the gorge area, to preserve and display the artefacts we had been seeing. My impressions of museums were of large rooms full of display cases, but they were clearly thinking on a much grander scale. They discussed some of the buildings that should be preserved and the sites that could be part of the museum area.

So this short course may have been when the inspiration for the huge Ironbridge Gorge Museum. The students seemed confident about acquiring the large amounts of money needed; I was very doubtful, but as things turned out they were right and I was wrong. But not even the most optimistic of them suggested the World Heritage Site concept. I still feel that some views of the gorge are dangerously near to delusions of grandeur.

It has been suggested that not only was this area the place where the Industrial Revolution started, it is also the home of Global Warming. The present scene is of a beautiful wooded valley with carefully restored buildings and tourist accommodation, of gentrified old houses and restaurants. What it commemorates is a stinking, polluted workplace full of sweating labourers from poor slums; it was an area of danger and fumes, spreading toxic gasses into the atmosphere. As a sort of encore we went off to Shrewsbury to look at Jones' Maltings, now known as the historic flax mill. Various efforts have since been made – and are still under way – to find the money to turn that into an historic attraction. Across the road was a Victorian cast-iron 'gents', which we thought a gem, though it's gone away now. That's a shame.

LIVING AND SHOPPING IN WELLINGTON BETWEEN THE WARS

Many Wrekin News readers have told me they like a bit of nostalgia, like the September article I wrote, so here is another dose for you. It's an attempt to portray life before the Last World War, but after the Great War To End All Wars as the 1914 to 1918 conflict was called, very ironically by old soldiers like my Dad, who also served in the 1939 – 45 war. This is not about either of the world wars but of the time between them. It is simply my own memories as one born in 1923, three years after the Versailles Treaty officially ended thee Great War, so a schoolboy of 16 when the Last World War started in 1939.

Between the wars Wellington had a great many more shops than now, though the population was less. Most of the shops were far smaller than now and there were a lot more people working in them. Before supermarkets swept through the country shoppers were used to being served, not to having to find the goods for themselves and queue to pay. For instance, Mum used to send me for the groceries to Lloyd's shop, where the Co-op bank is now, with a list and a basket. I sat down and handed the list to a girl assistant who went round the shop collecting the goods for me. Things like sugar, flour and tea would be weighed out from a large container and put in a paper bag, folded up neatly. Bacon was cut from a flitch. The cost of each item was added to Mum's list. Occasionally the girl might come to ask me about an item; usually I had no idea what Mum wanted and as I grew older this sometimes became an attempt to chat up the girl, which rarely worked.

When the list was complete the goods were piled into the shopping bag and I was presented with the bill. I had usually been given a pound note for a week's groceries for the four people in the family, so there was change in half crowns, florins, shillings, silver sixpences, pennies and halfpennies. By the time I was around sixteen there were few farthings or three-penny-bits used. The basket was then hung on the handlebars of my bike and I'd ride home.

There were things sold in the grocers' shops that we didn't buy. Dad grew most of our vegetables and fruit in the garden. Jam was made at home by Mum. Bread and milk were both delivered. The bread, by the way, was baked and delivered by Allan Frost's uncle. Our newspapers were delivered by Austin's from the shop in High Street that used to be Evans, Furnishers, over which I was born. Coal was also delivered for heating the house and cooking on a grate made in Ketley. It came in hundredweight bags and was often called Littleton nuts, usually from Gough's coal wharf at the goods station; the wharf was where Morrison's car park is now. Dad also bought timber from the Orleton estate, half a cord at a time, which I think was a pile six feet wide, four feet high and eleven feet long. We cut it up using a two man cross-cut saw and split it with a felling axe. It warmed us twice – once when cutting it up and once more on the fire.

Newspapers, when read, were for lavatory paper or fire lighters. Ash from the fire was spread on the garden paths to keep the weeds down. There was no plastic except for Bakelite, made from fish bones. Any left-over food was either fed to the birds or went on the compost heap together with weeds, prunings etc. Grass was cut with a hand propelled mower and unless very long was simply left on the lawn to rot down and fertilise the soil. Well-rotted compost was dug in the ground. We couldn't afford not to recycle.

In the living room was a Triplex grate which cooked our food, heated the water and warmed the room. It did all three jobs efficiently; Ketley was then, as now (Aga) a place for the latest in grate technology. The floor was in red tiles, probably from Blockley's of Hadley, who made some of the best. We were lucky enough to have a bathroom when I was twelve; before then we all had to share a small tin bath by the fire, one at a time, me first. The bathroom had been built on especially for us and was accessed from the kitchen, which is now probably against the regulations. Rainwater was collected from the roof into a big tank sunk into the ground by the back door; this was used for washing as it was soft water.

School uniform for the Boys' High School was supplied by Tom Grainger, a Methodist friend of my grandfather. The shop was in an old timber-framed building at the bottom of New Street, demolished in about 1960, resulting in the wider street in front of David Lloyd's jewellers. By then Tom had passed the shop on to his apprentice, Norman Jellyman. We wore black shoes, grey long socks, black shorts (until aged about 13) and a dark blue blazer. Our shirts were white, pullovers grey, and we wore dark blue school blazers and caps with either one, two or three light blue circles sewn on them, to show which house we were in. A narrow knitted tie was replaced by a cotton one later. Caps and blazers had school badges sewn on. The shorts had double thickness in the seat; long trousers replaced them when we were 14 or 15, by which time I was a man-sized boy.

At that time everybody shopped in Wellington. Much of the decline of local shops is due to local people shopping out of town, which is a pity. "If you don't want to lose it, use it" is a very good motto.

THE CALENDAR STONES ON THE WREKIN

WARNING – this story, though true, is hard to believe.

One day, many years ago, I was wandering on The Wrekin on my own. It was a sunny day. I had climbed down past the Cuckoo's Cup, or Raven's Bowl if you prefer, and noticed a patch of grass on my right, above a group of rocks. I sat down and studied the stones with interest. They looked rather odd; perhaps they had been put there for they didn't look like an outcrop. I looked on my map and tried to work out exactly what I was looking at. Perhaps it was something to do with light. For no reason at all I decided that something was going to happen there, and it would probably be at the next equinox in a few days' time. Probably it would happen at noon; that would be noon by the sun and we were ten minutes in time west of Greenwich so it'd be 12.10 by my watch.

I returned to the spot just before noon on the equinox and watched and waited. I was expecting that it would involve the gap between the two main stones. That turned out not to be so. At exactly the time I had calculated, 12.10, a shaft of light came through the right hand rock and formed a disc about the size of a twopenny coin on the small rock on the left. The light disc moved slowly, as the sun moved, for about ten minutes and disappeared.

Next day I returned but nothing happened. At the next equinox clouds obscured the sun, so there was nothing again. I have seen this happening several times over the years. The equinox, when our days and nights are exactly equal, occurs twice every year, in March and September. Several friends and members of my family have observed this little light show. Unfortunately I only once took a camera and brought home a picture, which I've lost. All I have is the watercolour sketch, included with this article, which proves nothing but at least it shows the stones as they were seen from my vantage point.

The stones look as if they have been moved here, a very difficult thing to do, and perhaps have been shaped. Are they the remains of some sort of building? Was it, perhaps some kind of temple? It could have been a building that was destroyed to eradicate the religion that had sprung from the stones. Early Christians were particularly good at getting rid of earlier beliefs. I'm reasonably sure there has been no archaeological investigation of the site so the only evidence is that of our own eyes. Of course we can use our imaginations but Wellingtonia is strictly non-fiction.

Think about the people who lived here, in the hillfort. They would have been able to construct a calendar from the equinox dates, which would have been very valuable for the farming community around. The phenomenon I have described would be seen as magic and the priests, shamans, or whoever kept this a secret, would be considered very great magicians. This could be proof that The Wrekin was a sacred mountain and give us a new reason for the hillfort being the tribal headquarters or capital of the land the Romans called Cornovia. But I can't prove anything.

For several years I have been unable to return to the site with my camera, so here's a challenge; I'm offering £20 for the first good, clear photograph of the light performing on the next equinox. Who'll win that?

CHURCH STREET, WELLINGTON

MEMORIES OF A VERY OLD STREET

Church Street is a place I have known for ninety years, though that is a very small part of its real age, which is at least measured in centuries if not millennia. The street is much older than the church, dated 1790 and older than the earlier church that was demolished before it. If I'm right this street existed long before the Domesday 'Walitone' of the early English and may have been a track before the Celts invaded. The mind boggles! I have a feeling that writing about my own memories of Church Street is going to be much easier than editing the kiloverb down to my limit of 1,000 words.

On the corner with Vineyard Road was a building we called 'the Doctor's shop', where we went for consultation with Dr Thomson, a dour Scot. To get an appointment you had to persuade the receptionist that you were in need of one, were given a number and sat waiting for a call. Dr Thomson used to tell women to always carry an umbrella with a sharp point so that she could fend off amateur first aiders until a doctor came. Several others joined the practice including Drs Bambridge and Hewatt-Jaboor. Eventually the building was sold to a building society, who added a fancy porch quite out of keeping.

Opposite was the old Police Station and Magistrates' Court; a fine old building, really solid and important. My school friend Bill Evans lived there. His father was the Inspector and had accommodation for his family at the back. We used to do our homework together in the courtroom on the first floor, on a big green baize table, and play table tennis afterwards. When the war started we helped sandbag the building to protect it from bombs. Later on I was one of the magistrates – ex officio as chairman of the Urban District Council. That was an experience, though as a very temporary member the other magistrates didn't take a lot of notice of me. When Telford came there was an enormous expansion of criminal activity; first the house was taken over for extra courts and then the whole court had a new building in Malinslee. I tried to buy it for the Town Council but we missed being able to buy it because of timing. It seems now to be an employment agency.

Next was once the Charlton Arms Hotel, a great shame now and I'd rather not comment because it's too annoying. Years ago the Murphy brothers owned it and it was promoted as the best hotel in town. There used to be a bowling green at the back but that went the way of many and became a car park. A large ballroom was built and many of the town's important functions were held there. The one I remember best was our Silver Wedding on 12th August (the date on which I'm writing this) in 1975. There was a heavy thunderstorm and the lights went out but we all thoroughly enjoyed ourselves. All sorts of famous and important people have stayed at the Charlton; I wonder if anyone has a guest list. Under the building are many cellars, where a lot of the history of Wellington could be discovered if it were properly investigated. What a great pity and a loss to our town.

The next building is an older police station, which once had the appropriate offices at the front and cells for detained prisoners at the back. Later it became the Conservative Party's headquarters, where many parties were held and of course local and national elections were organised. Later it was taken over by DB Roberts, estate agent.

After that comes an enigma. It's a car park of course, but should it be? Who owns it? The official answer is that nobody knows. The land is Wellington's ancient village green and it is not owned by T&W or by WTC. I remember in the 1950s discovering this enigmatic bit of land, when the grassed area was turned into a car park for the Westminster Bank (before NatWest) by the UDC. Before the Last World War there was a maypole, with children dancing around it, on May Day. In 1941 the Home Guard guarded a shot down German fighter plane as part of a propaganda exercise. The Green, its proper name, is, as best as we know owned by 'the people of Wellington. Some of us would like to see its restoration to its former status.

Across the road is the building that caused the formation of Wellington Civic Society. It was once an elegant place where there was a chemist's shop. Somehow a building society acquired the left hand half, demolished it, and built an ugly office, destroying its symmetry. Architect, Terry Stubbs, had his office in the old part and was disgusted that the new building had been permitted. We chatted and agreed that nobody was speaking up for Wellington's buildings and that Barclay's Bank should not have been allowed to demolish its Victorian gothic premises and replace it with an ugly modern one either. We called a meeting and the place was full of like-minded folks, so Wellington Civic Society was born in 1978.

The other side of Queen Street was once the home of the Wellington Journal and Shrewsbury News, owned by the Leake family, a very prosperous business with branches across Shropshire and Mid Wales. Then came the Post Office, later an outfitter and Arnold the Sadler who hand-made my school satchel. After Ten Tree Croft alley were solicitors. The Bacchus pub used to be called Dicky Parkes's for many years. Finally there is, as there has been for a very long time, Barbers, begun by John Barber who was the great entrepreneur whose Smithfield cattle auction was instrumental in Wellington's expansion from 1850n onwards. The furniture shop behind Barber's used to be the Morris Hall.

All Saints Church deserves its own kiloverb.

SOME NEW STREET SHOPS
BETWEEN 1935 AND 2015

Here's a little chat about the way in which a few of the shops in one small part of Wellington has changed over my own lifetime. It's an idea suggested by a friend who was talking about our constantly changing town. Some folk say that all this change is terrible but I suggest that change is inevitable and has been taking place constantly during the history of our town – or any other town for that matter. Some of the change is for the better and some for the worse; my own view is that, even though some of it is bound to be resented, especially by old people, a lot is for the better. Anyway, anything (or anybody) that doesn't change is on the way out.

I'm taking some of my information from the Wellington Directory of 1935, when I was 12, some from what I have seen recently and the rest is from my little old bald head. When I was about 12 we, the High School boys, used to ride down New Street on our bikes with cigarette packets in the wheel spokes that made quite a noise. We raced down on Thursdays – market days – thronged with shoppers. Very naughty it was. But nobody was hurt and we were not caught so we got away with it. I still come into Wellington but not on my bike.

Let's start at the bottom of New Street and look up. There's Greggs on the left and perhaps you have noticed that high up there's a built-in sign saying Lamb Inn. In 1935 the licensee was A. J. Rhodes. If you wish to know more about it as a pub, read Allan Frost's book. I remember a friend of mine, John Lovatt, who was manager of a grocery shop there in the 1950s. He told me the key to selling groceries in those days was cheap sugar – everybody wanted lots of it after wartime rationing. He discovered that the shop had a huge cellar, so he bought a ton of sugar cheap; word got around and he had many more customers. The sugar came in hundredweight sacks and was weighed into paper bags holding two pounds. Greggs seem to be doing well selling cakes and sandwiches.

Next was the Maypole Dairy which sold lots of butter and cheese. I remember them having beautifully sculptured butter on display in their window. That reminds me of the old story about a newly-rich woman who called margarine 'servants' butter', being very disparaging of both margarine and servants. She was described by a girl who had worked for her as a 'snooty old cow'. In the 1930s it was quite usual for girls to leave school at 14 and get a job working as a 'domestic'. Their employers need not have been at all rich themselves and the girls often stayed until they were married. A combination of the wartime jobs for women and labour saving gadgets changed things a lot.

Across the road was Melias Ltd. The grocers. There were very many grocers before supermarkets, dozens of them, all competing for the shopping of housewives who were looking for bargains. Each tried to have a more attractive manner, display and staff than the others. Boys had delivery bikes to save shoppers from having to carry their goods home. The bikes had a wire basket in front and could carry several parcels. The lads relied on tips from customers.

Next was a fine old Tudor oak framed building belonging to Tom Grainger, 'gents' outfitter', a Methodist friend of my grandfather. We went there for my school uniform; navy woollen stockings with light blue bands, grey shorts with double seat, navy blazer, knitted 'two blues' tie, two white shirts, navy school cap with two light blue circles for Ercall House and a navy gabardine mac. Everything was bought too big (he'll grow into it) and looked after very carefully until far too small. Men's shops smelled of pipe tobacco, women's shops of scent. It was very exciting buying uniform to start 'big school' and I remember it well.

Later the building was demolished, although of great historical importance because the beams had rotted and it was declared dangerous by Arthur Barton, the UDC engineer. He had been told to examine it and thrust a pen knife into a main beam; the blade, then the handle, then his thumb went straight into the rotted wood. He demanded and got a demolition order, which is why the street is wider here. Mrs Stilwell's Ladybird clothing shop next door had to be demolished too and she had the new building to face New Street; it's now David Lloyd's jewellery shop. Previously the road had been very narrow and turned sharply into the Square. Here the post coach swung sideways into a shop window so often that an iron bollard was put there to protect the window.

Next is the lovely little sweet shop, previously Rose, the butcher for a very long time, followed by Bill Jefferies, the baker. Then, after Bell Street is a corner shop now looking after beautiful ladies. It was Boffey's, confectioners in 1935 and at one time a lending library where, for a few pence you could borrow a novel, perhaps the 'trashy' sort Philip Larkin said he 'dished out to morons'. There was talk of the UDC demolishing this too and I was amused to find that the property owners were 'Feminine Adorables Ltd.'

Across the road were Maypole Dairy, B. Morrison, Hairdresser, Johnson Bros. (Dyers), London Central Meat, Craddock Bros, boot dealers and FR Burton, chemist. Now there's a 'bookie', Thai Restaurant and the lovely smelling Holland and Barrett, where I go for Soya milk substitute because cow's milk gives me bellyache. Oh the joys of old age!

Then comes Woolworth's in 1935. I could go on for pages about that but must stop now. We haven't got far, have we?

"Some folk say that all this change is terrible but I suggest that change is inevitable and has been taking place constantly during the history of our town – or any other town for that matter"

HOW OLD IS WELLINGTON?

AND OTHER QUESTIONS I CAN'T ANSWER

Often I am accosted by women –and men too – when I wander through the streets of Wellington Town Centre or sit at the edge of the Peace Garden. This is not in any way a complaint; in fact I rather enjoy it. They always start with the question of whether I'm the man who writes in Wrekin News and behave as if they already know the answer. Then comes the question that they'd always wanted to ask, but before they get a chance to ask it I jump in with, "I don't know the answer. What's the question?"

A common question is, 'How old is Wellington?' And I really don't know the answer to that one and neither does anyone else. "I've only been here 92 years," I say, "and it was certainly here when I came." Then we examine other people's answers. One local historian says it was the farm of the Angle or Saxon chap called Wealla or some such name. I'm sure he or someone else must have made it up.

Another historian tells us the Oxford Book of Place Names has it as a corruption of Weahleah-Ingaton, meaning 'the settlement round the temple in the grove'. He goes on to tell of Saxon or Angle mercenaries who fought for either the Romans or the Romanised Celts who took over the city of Viroconium after the legions had departed to defend Rome.

Other folks without degrees in history talk about Watlington because it was on the Watling Street (it wasn't) or the town with the wells (there are no towns without wells). By this time the whole thing is a bit confused.

Then I'm asked which one I think is right, and I reply, "None of them", which makes it worse. I believe that the name 'Walitone' in the Domesday Book of 1086 might be a clue and that the Wal part says it was Welsh (early English for foreigners) and that it was a settlement of some kind before the Angles made it part of England.

If my questioners haven't given up and gone away I say I'm basing my theory on the geological maps, which show parts of Wellington had post glacial soil, easy to plough or dig for the first farmers who came here and I reckon that is where they cleared a bit of forest and cultivated the land for crops. They didn't use the many local parts where there is 'boulder clay' as the geologists call it because it's very hard to cultivate.

The first explanation, Wealla, makes the town/village or more correctly settlement 1,200 years old, Weahleah Ingaton makes it nearer 1,400 years old and my own theory could be at least 6,000 years old. Of course it must have been a small settlement all those years ago and was not called Wellington because its occupants didn't speak English.

By the way, I reckon that Hadley, Ketley, Dawley, Madeley and several other local places may well be of similar ages. Some young whiz kid from Ironbridge was pontificating about 'the historic parts of Telford in Ironbridge' and asked why I was laughing. "Wellington had been a market town for a thousand years before anyone came up with the idea of building a bridge out of iron," I said.

Looking at geological and land use maps can give a good clue to a lot of history, though they are not used by many historians, who tend to rely on written documents. In Wellington, the area between Vineyard Road and Queen Street, Church Street and Bridge Road, with Charlton Street crossing the middle used to be a small lake, though there's no written evidence I know of. I have claimed it to be the town pond because it is a shallow depression lined with lake clay. There is evidence of the clay from those who have dug gardens and tranches for drainage. If you look carefully you'll find it to be like a saucer than would be a lake again without the drainage provided.

The land use maps show the untruths told by Telford Development Corporation who claimed (as some folk still do) that Telford was all built on pit mounds and slag heaps. That's not true. It was and is built almost entirely on agricultural land. If the original planners had done their research they'd have known this.

The Ironbridge Gorge is a great collection of museums and valuable exhibitions of industrial history but it's far from the only historic place around here. If everything in the World Heritage Site could be recreated it would have to include the foul stench of the coke furnaces the smell of burning animal bones for the bone china, the clouds of smoke from chimneys and factories and above all the grinding poverty of so many workers and their families, who often lived short, unhappy lives. Even Abraham's Darby family were short lived. Come to Ironbridge Gorge, the home of pollution and the destruction of a beautiful countryside. Ironbridge is the home of global pollution.

We are told all about the famous people but not of the men and women who actually did the work. Abraham Darby III did not build the Iron Bridge; he financed it, though he lost a lot of money and had to be rescued by Richard Reynolds of Ketley. Nobody knows the names of the men who actually did the job of building it. Far too much is known about the bosses and almost nothing about the workers.

Very often I encourage my questioners to go and find out for themselves the answers to their questions, even if they can't Google them and get instant answers (frequently wrong). Don't believe anything just because it's on your computer. There are plenty of places where you could research in old maps, geological maps and directories, some of which are in Wellington's excellent library and more in the Shrewsbury archives. Good hunting.

"I don't know the answer. What's the question?"